T0308524

LIVING AT FULL THROTTLE

Road Dog Publications was formed in 2010 as an imprint dedicated to publishing the best in books on motorcycling and adventure travel, by any means.

Visit us at www.roaddogpub.com.

No part of this book may be reproduced by any means, nor transmitted, nor translated into a machine language, without the written permission of the publishers.

Living at Full Throttle
Copyright © 2024 Kathleen Terner
All rights reserved.

Photo on page 105 courtesy of Gary Medin

Iron Butt, Iron Butt Association, Saddlesore, and Bun Burner are registered service and trademarks.

All Scripture quotations are taken from the Holy Bible, New International Version®, NIV®. Copyright ©1973, 1978, 1984, 2011 by Biblica, Inc.™ Used by permission of Zondervan. All rights reserved worldwide. www.zondervan.com. The "NIV" and "New International Version" are trademarks registered in the United States Patent and Trademark Office by Biblica, Inc.™

ISBN 978-1-890623-93-7
Library of Congress Control Number: 2024938570

An Imprint of Lost Classics Book Company
This book also available in eBook format at online booksellers. ISBN 978-1-890623-94-4

LIVING AT FULL THROTTLE

WHAT WOULD YOU DO IF FEAR WERE NOT YOUR FIRST THOUGHT?

by

Kathleen Terner

Publisher
Lake Wales, Florida

Dedicated to

My children: Ethan, Elliot, and Eleanor

For inspiring me to move beyond my fear and for affirming me in learning to live and love more fully.

ABOUT THE AUTHOR

After receiving positive feedback on her first book, *Two-Wheeled Wind Therapy*, published in 2021, Kathleen Terner sought advice from loved ones about when to pen a second book. Her daughter wisely noted, "Mom, it's not every year that you have a life-changing epiphany. Wait until you have something new to write about." Taking Eleanor's advice to heart, Kathleen focused on living out what she had already put to paper, looking for more ways to grow as a person, and sharing her inspiring message through public speaking opportunities.

Of course, she also hit the road, learning more life lessons through her motorcycle travels to all forty-eight contiguous states, up through Alaska to the Arctic Ocean, and across Canada to Newfoundland.

The unexpected medical news she received in June of 2023 put her philosophy of asking "What would you do if fear were not your first thought?" to the test. Her response to this challenging report gave her greater clarity about the ways we can all respond to fear from a position of power instead of powerlessness. It also heightened her awareness about the importance of living each day at "Full Throttle."

Kathleen is the proud mother of three adult children, has taught high school math for almost twenty years, is active in her church and community, and has a thriving tutoring business that has helped finance her motorcycle travels to twenty-four countries.

CONTENTS

This ride along the Cascade Scenic Highway, originally planned with two of my favorite riding partners, had to be postponed for a week after receiving unexpected news from my radiation oncologist.

PROLOGUE

AN UNEXPECTED CALL

When the phone rang at 3:30 in the afternoon on Friday, June 2, 2023, I was just packing up my things. It had been a busy week at work, teaching my high school students geometry and advanced algebra, and I was looking forward to a motorcycle ride to the Cascade Scenic Highway with two of my favorite riding partners the next morning.

The call from my doctor at Oregon Health and Sciences University was rather unexpected. I had met with him just two weeks before and gotten the good news that the throat cancer I had battled three years earlier still appeared to be in remission. At that appointment, I had mentioned struggling with double vision and agreed to get an MRI to rule out any issues with my brain, intending to check that concern off my list before leaving with my motorcycle on a summer trip to Iceland and several other European countries.

But when I picked up the call and Dr. Jason Burton asked me, "Has anyone called you to discuss your MRI?" time stood still. My heart rate accelerated, I felt pressure building up in my ears, and the desks in my classroom seemed to fade away. The sound of the blood rushing to my head almost drowned out his next words, and I had to sit down to hear what he had to say. "No," I replied, with my hands shaking, "What did you find?" Dr. Burton explained that the MRI had picked up four tumors in my brain, some of which were located near my eye socket and the muscles to my eye. It was possible that my prior cancer had metastasized to my brain, that I had a cancer of the fluid surrounding my brain, that I had another new form of cancer, or that the tumors were benign.

When confronted with such stark news a few years before, I might have crumpled over my desk and cried. But over the last three years I had learned, through a variety of life-changing motorcycle adventures, to see myself more as a person of strength. I had also developed a deeper awareness of God's abundant grace and provision for me. (*footnote*) So, although the call was not anticipated, I knew that I was prepared to face the challenge head on. I took a deep breath, grabbed a piece of paper from my bookshelf to write on, and asked Dr. Burton, "What are our next steps?"

I realize that not everyone reading this book shares my faith. I've mentioned it at points where it played an essential role in my story, and I appreciate the reader's openness to me sharing from my heart in this way.

My summer 2020 solo cross-country ride to visit my older son in Washington, DC, ended up being a life changing adventure as I learned to experience confidence, joy, and hope again after battling throat cancer and surviving a second divorce.

CHAPTER 1

DREAMS BEYOND THE DRIVEWAY

There are few times, if ever, when something we experience over the course of a few seconds permanently alters the trajectory of our lives. However, my life-or-death moment in the muddy ruts of the Dalton Highway returning from the Arctic Ocean the summer before I had received that call had forever changed my understanding of God's power, as well as my perception of my own strength in dealing with extraordinary difficulties.

The decision to travel up to the Arctic had not been an easy one, as the Dalton itself is considered one of the most dangerous roads in the world, and I was a relatively inexperienced rider. I had received my motorcycle endorsement at the age of fifty-two, only three years before in 2018, and even as late as 2020 I was still too afraid to ride my 700-pound Harley up my steep driveway out of my garage.

At 5'1" tall and slight of build, I had felt fairly intimidated by such a large machine. I had always been more of a bookworm and less of an athlete, staying up late at night reading under the covers of my bed at only five years of age, my hazel eyes framed by glasses and my small forehead furrowed in concentration. I had made brief attempts at participating in sports as a youngster. But when I failed to make a single shot during a game playing basketball in junior high and then falling off the balance beam in a short stint at gymnastics, getting the wind knocked out of me so I couldn't breathe, I decided sports were not for me.

I had failed my first skills test when trying to obtain a motorcycle endorsement, after my passion for the sport had been ignited by years of travel on the back of my then-husband's bike. I had done reasonably well during the training session conducted by Team Oregon, but when it came time to do the test, I had a panic attack, driving over the cones instead of around them, failing to brake in time, and riding outside the lines when trying to corner.

I was mortified by my spectacular failure but determined not to give up, as I yearned for the independence of having my own bike. After taking two more private lessons from a patient instructor, I managed to pass the skills test on my second try a week after my initial attempt, earning the lowest possible passing score. With my license in hand, I started to practice on my first bike, a Honda Rebel 250, riding 4,000 miles in the first few months I owned it. What I lacked in skill I made up for in passion, loving every minute I felt the wind in my face, the rumble of the bike, and the texture of the road.

I soon transitioned to my next bike, a used 2018 Harley-Davidson Softail Slim with a mighty Milwaukie-Eight 107 engine, that fit me perfectly. Its low twenty-six-inch seat height and custom raised handlebars made it possible for me to put both feet flat on the ground and easily reach the handgrips. Thrilled with the power and ease with which I roared up and over hills, around corners, and down straightaways, I soon dubbed the bike "My Baby."

Although I loved piloting the bike on the open road, learning to get the machine up my steep driveway was a different matter. I was concerned I might tip it over if I did not ride up the incline fast enough or slip out into my busy street if I opened up the throttle too much. Even a year and a half after obtaining my license, I still relied on my husband to get the bike out of the garage for me, as I was too afraid to do it myself.

At that time, in the winter of 2020, I was struggling with fears on multiple fronts, fighting stage two throat cancer and facing a failing marriage. As the hair on the back of my head fell out from the chemo treatments, I lost the ability to speak or eat due to the side effects of the radiation, and had to program a speech app to talk for me in the classroom, I remained in what was a verbally, emotionally, and physically abusive situation because I was too afraid to live alone and was worried that God would not forgive me for a second divorce. My husband's betrayals weighed heavily on me, and I did not think I could ever experience joy again.

But while battling cancer and facing death in the eye, all three of my children had come to me independently to beseech me to get a divorce, telling me lovingly but firmly that they would not allow their future children to visit me if my husband was still in the house. As I pondered their thought-provoking comments, I realized that I might not have long left to live and did not want my children's last memories of me to be ones of me cowering in fear.

The next several months were transformational as I completed my cancer treatments, filed the paperwork for a second divorce, and made the life-changing decision to head off on a solo eight-week cross country motorcycle trip to visit my older son in Washington, DC, learning to experience confidence, joy, and hope again. Over the course of two months and more than 15,000 miles, I traveled on some of the most technically challenging roads in the country and completed several nested, certified Iron Butt Association rides, on two occasions traveling over 1,500 miles in less than thirty-six hours. That summer adventure helped me start to see myself as a person of value and strength, someone willing to take on challenges and to ask myself what steps I might take if fear were not my first thought.

I had also learned that God had more grace for me than I ever imagined, offering me forgiveness and hope instead of condemnation. While I had spent years fixated on my mistakes and failures, he had been focusing on the character he wanted to develop in me. When I had felt defeat and hopelessness, he had been offering me a fresh beginning. As I saw myself through a lens of shame, he was gazing at a beautiful daughter whom he loved. Although the trials and tribulations of my past had indeed shaped who I was to some extent, I was beginning to understand that they did not have to define me. It was up to me to determine the future I wanted to plot for myself.

In the summer of 2021, I headed east again, filled with confidence in the new person I was becoming and excited about exploring my limits. Having just published my first memoir, *Two-Wheeled Wind Therapy* (**footnote**) about the positive life lessons I had learned on the road, I arranged for book signings in each of the four corners of the US— Washington, Maine, Florida, and California.

Initially interested in visiting the twenty states in the lower forty-eight I hadn't made it to the summer before, I soon realized I didn't want to miss any of my favorite spots in the other twenty-eight states either. Over the eight-and-a-half weeks of my summer adventure, I ended up riding almost 23,000 miles through all forty-eight contiguous United States and completing several additional certified, nested Iron Butt Association rides, including traveling over 2,000 miles in less than forty-eight hours. I arrived home at summer's end happy with the extent to which I had challenged myself and full of

Available on the Shop tab at www.kathleenterner.com.

even more hope and confidence than when I began the trip. Through my motorcycle adventures, I was beginning to see the magnitude of what I could accomplish when I stopped focusing on all the reasons why I couldn't pursue a dream and instead asked myself what my action steps might look like.

In thinking through options for my summer 2022 adventure, I yearned to stretch my wings a little further beyond the forty-eight states I had already visited. With some COVID travel restrictions being lifted and the borders to Canada open for the first time in years, I looked at the map and was intrigued with the idea of making it all the way north through Canada and Alaska to Prudhoe Bay and the Arctic Ocean, the northernmost point in the United States accessible by road. There was something extremely compelling to me about traveling to the far reaches of North America at the same time I was beginning to stretch and grow as a person.

My burgeoning confidence on the road had been mirrored by increasing success in my personal life. I had found that when I viewed myself as a person of value it was easier for me to have healthy relationships with the people closest to me.

In the Spring of 2022, while contemplating journeying to Alaska, I had a difficult conversation with a family member whom I love deeply. During our talk, he made some broad-sweeping negative generalizations about me. In the past, I would have responded out of hurt and fear, asking for reassurance regarding my worth to him. Not this time.

I gave him a broad smile and cheerfully commented, "I've got great news for you! I'm not the same person I used to be. I can respect myself, regardless of what you might say about me. What that means is that instead of responding to you in an emotional manner and escalating this conversation, you and I are going to be able to calmly discuss our options and have a good rest of our evening together." He looked at me, cocked his head sideways, and paused, apparently not sure what to say next. After taking a breath, he admitted, "I guess I was exaggerating." We left that conversation with a resolution to our issue, but more importantly with mutual respect.

Reflecting on the successful outcome to what could have been a drama-filled evening, I was grateful that some of the wisdom and maturity I had gained through my trips had helped me to respond more positively to my loved one at home. So, as I contemplated traveling to the northernmost tip of this country, I was not only thinking about my next motorcycle adventure but also wanting to find a way to commemorate the significance of the healthy changes I had made in my personal life. The more I thought about the beauty of Alaska, the challenge of the ride up to the Artic, and the significance of achieving such a major milestone, the more I felt I owed it to myself to at least attempt to reach Prudhoe Bay.

Shortly after posting my plans to travel to Alaska on Facebook, I received messages from riders all over the world telling me why I should consider changing my plans. They were concerned that there wasn't enough gas, there were too many bears, I was a woman, I was traveling alone, and the roads were treacherous. Well-meaning bikers shared horror stories of totaled bikes, aborted trips, and dangerous conditions with no help in sight.

One particularly passionate plea came from a fellow female motorcyclist with much more experience than I who had traveled to Prudhoe Bay, also known as Deadhorse, several times before. She urged me to reconsider my plans, warning me that the Dalton highway, the only route from Fairbanks to Deadhorse "is a seriously uncompromising road for inexperienced riders" and that "courage is not what you need to defeat it. Accommodation is very limited, serious weather can happen unexpectedly at any time, we had snow in June over Atigun Pass, and if it rains, the unpaved section turns to gritty porridge fifteen inches deep and the trucks don't give to motorcyclists, they treat us with contempt at best. It is not a road to ride alone. Rescue is virtually nonexistent and don't even think of stopping on the road."

Although I was initially a little taken aback by her intensity, I carefully considered her warnings and realized there was much substance to her concerns and those expressed by others. The Dalton Highway, often referred to as the "Haul Road," covers 500 miles of mostly dirt and gravel road with few services, extreme weather, limited communication with the outside world, and heavy semi-truck traffic, with big rigs carrying supplies and equipment back and forth from the oil fields up north. In fact, renting an adventure-type bike for the arduous trip north through companies in Fairbanks or Anchorage came with a $600 to $1,000 surcharge to cover damage to the frame and tires that was often associated with the treacherous road.

As I pondered how to respond to the challenges of a trip north, I thought about my personal journey over the last couple of years and what it signified regarding my travel plans. Just two years earlier, when I had been filled with shame and hopelessness over my deteriorating marriage, I had sometimes spent hours a day crying on the bathroom floor, with a towel covering my face to muffle the sounds of my sobs from my children's ears. I felt completely trapped and powerless, unable to survive the toll the abuse and betrayals were taking on my mental and physical health but unwilling to get a second divorce, thinking that God could forgive me for one failed marriage but not two. I was ashamed by what I had allowed to happen and isolated myself from others. From my perspective, my problems were too insurmountable for even God to fix. With no perceived hope for my future in sight and no strength to continue, I prayed regularly for God to take me in my sleep.

When I had finally reached rock bottom, I cried out to God, telling him I realized I was completely powerless to remedy my situation, trying to fix things on my own was not working, and I was willing to do whatever he asked of me, even if that meant living alone the rest of my life and being ostracized by others because of my mistakes.

To my complete and utter shock, I had discovered over the intervening months that God had so much more hope to offer me than I ever thought possible. I had envisioned being rejected by people because of my failures but instead found that it was easier to connect with them when I was open about my shortcomings. I didn't see how I would make new friends at my later stage in life but discovered a whole community of fellow bikers willing to give me advice about my bike and to spend time with me on rides. Although living at home alone was an adjustment at first, I found myself so much calmer when I wasn't worried about my bedroom door being kicked open, being physically or verbally assaulted, or being rocked by the news of yet another betrayal.

Instead of the loneliness and isolation I expected after my second divorce, I found myself making new friends with fellow bikers, including these two treasured riding companions, L-R Grant Myers and Leo Guzman Fernandez.

I hadn't thought I was brave enough to live by myself, let alone travel across the country by motorcycle on my own. But as I became more aware of God's presence in my life and more willing to surrender entirely to Him, I had found within me an inner strength and fortitude I never imagined possible. Ironically, it was when I was finally willing to give up full control of my situation that I began to really see the power God had in my life.

So, as I pondered how to respond to the concerns raised by others about a ride to the Arctic, I realized the only relevant question to me was whether I felt God calling me to make the trip. I had thought all along that my story and the pain I had endured somehow might be used to inspire and encourage others facing similar challenges. I understood that on my own I was not capable of making it to Prudhoe Bay and back but that with divine help anything was possible. I also believed that undertaking such an adventure after experiencing so much failure in my personal life would be a tangible testament to the power we can experience when we give our lives wholly to God.

The more I prayed and thought about it, the more I realized that I was no longer the woman crying on the bathroom floor, afraid and alone. I was not mired in feelings of shame and worthlessness but instead buoyed by the grace and provision so kindly shown me. I was no longer terrified to ride up my steep driveway but had, in fact, traveled to all forty-eight states by motorcycle by myself. Although I was still a relatively inexperienced rider and had no idea how I would find an affordable bike to ride up the Dalton on a teacher's salary, I resolved I would rather try to ride to Prudhoe Bay and fail than not try because I might fail. Now I just had to figure out how to make it happen.

With forty fatalities a year on the Dalton Highway, I wasn't sure if I would be returning home to my children after my attempt to reach the Arctic Ocean. The heartfelt notes I penned before my departure conveyed my love to them in case I was no longer able to express it in person.

CHAPTER TWO

PLANNING FOR PRUDHOE

Having received so much input from others regarding the hazards of a ride up the Dalton, I began to think of specific ways I could prepare for such a grueling journey. I purchased bear spray and extra gas cans, rented a SAT phone capable of communicating from anywhere on earth, obtained a GPS tracking device with a emergency SOS button, researched potential routes and gas stops on the way north, got more advice from others who had traveled to Alaska, downloaded the app needed to pass through Canadian customs, and participated in a dirt bike training camp to become more familiar with riding on dirt and gravel.

Finding a bike to take to the Arctic proved to be one of the most daunting aspects of the preparation. Although I planned to ride my Harley to Alaska, I wasn't comfortable riding it up the Haul Road to Prudhoe Bay because of the damage it might incur, as well as the fact it was not designed for dirt and gravel.

I could not afford the hefty surcharges levied by formal bike rental companies in either Fairbanks or Anchorage and hoped to find a private individual willing to loan me their bike through one of the available riders share rental apps.

After weeks of searching for up to two hours a day, I still didn't have any viable leads. In May of 2022, I finally connected with James Siegel in Anchorage, Alaska, a blogger who had followed my adventures and was willing to rent me his Kawasaki Versys-X 300 if I fully insured it for complete replacement and provided extra funds to cover some of the wear and tear on the bike when I returned. Although the bike was equipped with seventy percent on-road/thirty percent off-road tires designed primarily for pavement, not knobby tires ideal for loose gravel and dirt, it was the best option I had.

Although I knew I had done my best to prepare for my trip, I also understood that, with an average rate of forty fatal crashes a year on the Dalton, there was a possibility I would not return. Feeling led to take on the dangers of the journey but not wanting to overly alarm my children by having a conversation that might easily be perceived as final loving words before I left, I decided to leave them heartfelt notes conveying everything I would want them to know if I were no longer able to be with them.

Before heading north, I wrote a lengthy, deeply personal letter to each of my children, telling them how much they meant to me, how grateful I was to them for standing by me through the trials of the last few years, how proud I was of them, and how optimistic I was about their future. It was important to me that I conveyed my love for them as clearly as possible, in case I was not able to do so myself later. Although I knew there were inherent risks to the trip I was taking, I was also hopeful that successfully facing such a daunting challenge would allow me to return to them an even stronger version of myself. Little did I know how transformational my journey would end up being!

Everything in Alaska appeared larger than life, from the snow-topped mountains towering over blue bodies of water, to the ragged wading pool sized potholes in the road, to the swarms of mosquitos buzzing relentlessly around my face shield.

CHAPTER THREE

ALASKA OR BUST

I felt a palpable sense of excitement as I tightened the straps on my luggage in my garage the morning of June 18, 2022, preparing to begin my summer journey north with a trip across the Peace Arch border into Canada later that day. After nineteen months of COVID-related restrictions on travel, the country had just opened its borders for non-essential motorists a few months before. I had submitted all the necessary documentation earlier via the ArriveCAN app and was thrilled to be traveling to another country for the first time on my motorcycle.

Although I didn't know exactly what adventures awaited me in the days ahead, I anticipated that there would be many more firsts. The stories I had heard about the hazardous road surfaces, dangerous wildlife, and spectacular views of nature in the north painted a picture of extreme conditions and breathtaking beauty. To ameliorate the risks associated with the scarcity of gas and lodging, I had carefully plotted a course north along the Stewart-Cassiar Highway through British Columbia, then west on the Alcan Highway through the Yukon and into Alaska, making careful notes regarding fuel supplies and overnight accommodations.

Normally I wouldn't dream of putting regular gas in my bike, but, as this sign at a fuel station in the Yukon Territory made abundantly clear, my options heading north were limited.

I soon discovered that the tales I had heard about the challenges of travel to Alaska were not exaggerations. The further I pushed north, the more difficult the ride became, with mud-filled potholes in the road the size of children's wading pools and cracks and crevasses large enough to swallow a chihuahua. Mosquitoes were out in full force, swarming relentlessly around my face when I stopped at gas stations with limited offerings for fuel or food. I was grateful to have a gaiter, helmet, and goggles to protect my ears, mouth, nose, eyes, and forehead from the relentless insects sometimes jokingly referred to as "Alaska's state bird."

I began to understand the enormity of the adventure in front of me when I traveled from the small town of Smithers, British Columbia, up to Dease Lake on the fourth day of my trip. Leaving my hotel in Smithers, dwarfed by the massive granite Hudson Bay Mountains towering over the city, I saw a flashing red electronic warning sign above me, alerting me to the fact the road leading to my destination for the night was submerged in three feet of water. Not sure how else I could get to Dease Lake, I decided to forge ahead in the heavy rain and deal with any obstacles as they presented themselves.

Just a few miles before my fuel stop in Meziadin Junction that day, I rounded a corner to discover a large brown bear standing in my lane. With only a split second to decide whether to attempt a U-turn or pass by, I elected to speed up and skirt around the animal, reasoning that I would have a higher likelihood of outrunning it at higher speeds than if I slowed to turn around. I wasn't sure whether to be terrified or thrilled but couldn't help laughing as I sped away.

As I continued traveling north and west through British Columbia and up through the Yukon territory, I passed through stunning mountain ranges that left me wondering if I was heading to Alaska or on vacation in the Swiss Alps. I navigated around more bears, traveled through rain heavy enough to fill up the insides of my goggles, and bumped and jostled my way along gravel and dirt roads under construction. On one particularly trying stretch of dirt, a semi passed me going the other direction, sending a large plume of dust my way that completely obscured my view of the road and gave new meaning to the term *flying blind*. I pointed my bike in the direction the road had been and prayed no one would hit me.

Five days and over 2,000 miles after leaving home, I crossed into Alaska at the Beaver Creek Checkpoint, delighted to have finally reached the forty-ninth state after years of dreaming of such an accomplishment. I stopped for the night at Copper Creek, making it a point to kill all the mosquitos in my rustic cabin before laying my head down for the night. Arriving in Anchorage the next day, I headed straight to the dealership to drop off My Baby for a much-needed service, as the rough roads had already loosened the bike's left turn signal, compromised two of the power sources for my navigation, and covered the entire bike with a thick crust of dirt and grime. Later that evening, with my Harley safely tucked away in my host family's garage, I began to prepare for my departure the next morning on my rented bike for the almost 900-mile ride to Fairbanks and along the Dalton Highway to Deadhorse Camp in Prudhoe Bay on the Arctic.

Made it! After traveling by bike through all forty-eight contiguous states on multiple occasions in the past, nothing could wipe the grin off my face after I finally reached the forty-ninth state after years of dreaming of such an achievement.

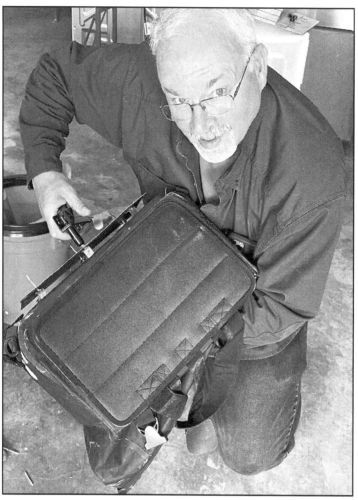

Dan came to my rescue, jury-rigging a barrier to protect my right pannier bag from the heat of my exhaust pipe after I discovered a hole that could have caused an explosive situation.

CHAPTER 4

DEPARTING FOR THE DALTON

Organizing my gear to head north, I discovered the first of several problems with my equipment. The owner of my rental bike had kindly purchased pannier bags for me to use, but when I picked up the bike, we discovered they could not be attached. Fortunately, I had mailed backup bags and extra straps to my host home in Anchorage, as it was essential that I be able to carry the water, food, clothing layers, and extra gas required for the Haul Road. I was concerned the bags were riding lower than I would have liked. But, hoping to avoid a costly last-minute purchase, I cinched them up as tightly as I could and loaded everything up.

Shortly after leaving Anchorage the next morning, I realized that the rigid phone mount attached to the bike apparently had not adequately dampened the motorcycle's vibrations from the rough road, and my iPhone emitted a buzzing sound anytime I tried to open the camera. Although the navigation feature still appeared to be functional, I was concerned that the phone might not survive the harsh conditions on the current mount during the rest of the ride to the Arctic. After pulling the bike over to contact Apple support, I realized I might need to replace both the phone and the mount the next morning.

Determined to enjoy the day's ride, I focused on what I could identify of the Denali Mountain Range behind the thick layer of smoke from the many wildfires then blazing in the state. While at a gas station near the entrance to Denali National Park, I received an evacuation warning on my phone and decided not to linger.

In hindsight, I could not have been more fortunate that I had planned to stay with fellow bikers in Fairbanks, because the pannier bags ended up becoming a bigger issue than I had anticipated. Dan and Carol Schwietert welcomed me, fed me a delicious home-cooked meal, prayed for my safety over the next several days, loaned me a flexible phone mount, and gave me timely tips regarding some of the hazards of the road I would be riding on the next four days.

After replacing my phone the next morning, I walked out to my bike in the parking lot, hoping to start the day's 250-mile journey to Coldfoot Camp, the halfway point between Fairbanks and Deadhorse, only to discover the exhaust pipe had burned a hole in my right pannier. Since each of my bags contained two gas canisters, I knew the issue had to be addressed immediately—excessive heat near the fuel could result in an explosive situation. I returned to the Schwietert's house, where Dan was able to fashion a barrier for the pannier out of sheet metal and attach it to the bottom of my bag, sending me on my way with a cheerful smile and a wave, his blue eyes twinkling behind his glasses and his skin rosy from the hot afternoon sun.

One of many challenges of riding the Dalton "Haul Road" is the scarcity of gas on the 500-mile stretch between Fairbanks and Deadhorse, making this pump in Yukon River Camp a highly treasured resource.

CHAPTER 5

HEADING UP THE HAUL ROAD

Shortly afterward, I posed at the welcome sign for the Dalton Highway, full of anticipation and joy that my journey up the infamous road was finally beginning. I think I had been so focused on preparing for the trip that I had somewhat forgotten the extent of the difficulties I would be facing. When two other visitors at the sign, traveling by four-wheel Jeep, commented on how brave I must be to travel alone by motorcycle on the road, it reminded me of the seriousness of my situation. Then, as I pointed the bike north, I passed a group of about six large men on well-equipped adventure bikes, completely covered from head to toe in caked dirt. I remembered the warnings I had heard about construction equipment spraying the road, creating a slippery, hazardous riding surface.

Determined to keep heading toward the Arctic Ocean, I journeyed on, quickly learning that standard rules regarding road construction did not apply to the Haul Road. At home in the lower forty-eight, even small pockets of dirt and gravel in the road were accompanied by several staggered orange warning signs and often surrounded by cones. On the Dalton, the surface regularly switched between gravel, dirt, and pock-marked pavement with no warning, often after the crest of an incline when visibility was low. After having to brake suddenly several times and coming perilously close to dumping the bike, I learned to head up rises cautiously.

A brief conversation with visitors at this iconic sign reminded me of the dangers that lay ahead of me as I traveled north on this hazardous road.

The hills were extraordinary, with steep inclines and downgrades the likes of which I had not seen since I was a little girl traveling on the roads of San Francisco in the back of my mom's VW wagon. With an abundance of both dust and water in my path on the Dalton, I felt like I was riding an old roller coaster up and down a series of big hills, through a variety of dirt and water features. One of the key technical challenges became learning to navigate the treacherous surface while at the same time being hit by the dirt, mud, and rocks thrown up by passing trucks.

On one occasion, a large construction vehicle emerged over the rise of a hill, heading toward me in my lane, pushing a large mound of loose soil. He made no attempt to slow down as I narrowly avoided being buried in the dirt by skirting to the side on the shoulderless road.

Farther down the Haul Road, I discovered that the hills next to me were on fire. I could see several walls of flames shooting down the incline toward me, and as I progressed down the road, the blaze was just a few yards away. Sure that at any time a firefighter would appear, ordering me to turn around, I sped up the bike, hoping not to be stopped.

I was thrilled to reach Coldfoot Camp later that evening. The promise of both gas and hot food made the loose collection of rudimentary, weather-beaten trailers seem like a five-star hotel. I filled up my tank at the lone pump in the large gravel parking lot and polished off three plates of food at the all-you-can-eat buffet, happy to have a warm place to stay for the night before continuing another 240 miles north to Deadhorse in the morning.

Jubilant to have made the halfway point between Fairbanks and Deadhorse and ravenous from the day's ride, I posed with my mud-encrusted rental bike before heading into the camp cafeteria.

After a large breakfast the next day, I continued up the Dalton, feeling more confident with the road conditions and heavy semi traffic than I had the day before. When I stopped for my first break, I noticed that my tire had worn a hole in my left pannier, shearing off the arm of one of my three essential clothing layers and destroying an electric glove. I patched the bag together with more straps, saved the pieces of the torn riding hoodie to be patched back together later, and got back on the bike, happy to be that much closer to Prudhoe Bay.

I felt a palpable sense of adventure as I traveled alone down the Dalton, sighting a red fox with a fresh kill and a huge musk ox with long, mangy fur foraging by the side of the road. I passed ice-covered lakes and traversed over Atigun Pass, at an elevation of 4,822 feet, the highest route in Alaska open year-round. The snow-covered peaks glistened in the summer sun, the cold air turned my cheeks red, and I thought to myself, "Wow! I really am riding to the Arctic."

Ice and snow on the sides of the road and covering the mountain peaks above me were tangible reminders that I was nearing the Arctic Ocean when I stopped here in June at the highest Alaskan pass open year-round.

One of the unique challenges of the stretch of road between Coldfoot Camp and Prudhoe Bay was the absence of any restrooms or pullouts. My strategy for taking care of business was to stop on a flat section, listen to see if I could hear traffic coming from either direction, and then do what I needed to do as quickly as possible. On one occasion close to the end of the day, I misjudged the situation and was passed by two male bikers before I had gotten back on the bike. I remember thinking as they rode past, "Hopefully, I won't see them again." The thought was short-lived, as I ended up passing them just a few miles down the road. Not sure what to do, I gamely waved as I went by, hoping that perhaps I had been mistaken and they hadn't seen anything after all. My mind turned away from the potentially embarrassing moment and focused instead on reaching Deadhorse.

I survived! Jumping for joy before plunging into the freezing Arctic waters, I was so thrilled to have made it safely to Prudhoe Bay.

CHAPTER 6

PRUDHOE BAY AT LAST!

Riding into Prudhoe Bay that evening was surreal. I had dreamed of the moment for months, hoping to reach the northernmost point of the United States accessible by road, but never sure how far I would get. I had outrun fires, skirted around bears, dodged semi-trucks and construction vehicles, navigated treacherous surfaces with no services in sight, and forged forward with two destroyed pannier bags and clothing layers on an unfamiliar bike.

I had always known it was possible I might face a trip-ending failure with my gear or bike on the Haul Road journey but was hopeful that I would at least reach Deadhorse first. I felt a palpable sense of relief to pull into the small working enclave of oil company employees and support personnel, fill up my gas at the only pump in town, and check in to the Deadhorse Camp cluster of trailers for dinner and lodging.

As one of just a few guests staying at the austere working camp, it was easy to spot the three other bikers, all men on adventure bikes, two of whom I had encountered earlier during my bathroom mishap. Mike Douthitt, a tall, burly retired pharmacist from Butte Montana with sparkling hazel eyes, and his riding companion, Bradley Murfitt, an affable clean-shaven Seargent at Arms for the State of Montana, kindly did not mention passing me in the middle of my pit stop earlier in the day. Mike and Brad had neighboring summer cabins in Montana and had started planning their Alaska trip together in 2020 while Brad was recovering from knee surgery. Hardy Patel, a friendly, talkative software engineer from Fremont, California, with deep brown eyes and a closely cropped black mustache and beard, was traveling separately but had met the two other men earlier that day on their way north. Hardy had chosen to use his ten-year anniversary sabbatical from eBay to travel solo up to Deadhorse after discovering in 2017 that he loved the sense of freedom from traveling on his own by motorcycle.

Although our little group had just formed over dinner, it felt like we had known each other for ages as we laughed together about the mishaps and obstacles we had faced earlier on the Dalton, giddy with excitement about safely reaching Prudhoe Bay. There was an easy camaraderie among us as we shared stories of our motorcycle adventures over the years, as well as our hopes and dreams for future trips.

We were all booked on a tour to the Arctic Ocean the next day, as access to that body of water is controlled by the oil companies and available only to those who had provided identification and obtained permission ahead of time. I hadn't realized that I would have the option to swim in the frigid water and had not packed a swimsuit, but an oil worker at the camp loaned me his thin, white long-sleeved T-shirt, and I decided it would have to do. I wasn't going to pass up an opportunity to submerge myself in the Arctic the next morning!

After dinner, my heart bursting with joy from the day's successes, I called all three of my children to tell them I had safely reached Prudhoe Bay. My older son, Ethan, suggested I check my motorcycle tires for damage. I was hesitant to do so at first, knowing that there were no motorcycle repair shops in the little town. Flush with excitement about making it all the way up the Dalton, I hoped that my luck would hold out enough for me to return to Fairbanks and the relative safety of the larger town with all the services it provided.

However, Ethan insisted I do a safety check, and I knew it was important for me to listen to him. I have a great deal of respect for my son, as he is quite articulate, intelligent, and accomplished. It has been such a gift to see him grow into a young man and to realize that, as he has aged and matured, our relationship has shifted. When he was younger, it was my responsibility to impart wisdom and protect him. But as we have both gotten older, he has taken on a protective role in my life, often advising me of ways to stay safe or make wise decisions. With a smile on his face, a shake of the thick blond hair on his head, and a pat on my back with his muscular arms, he would often steer me in the right direction. So, while the exhausted part of me felt like hiding my head in the sand, I knew his suggestion was appropriate and that, at the very least, I needed to take a quick look at the bike.

After hanging up, I walked out to my motorcycle, hoping a cursory inspection of the portion of my tires not covered by the fenders or frame of the bike would reveal no problems. Imagine my surprise when, on the few inches of rubber visible to me in the dusk of the Alaskan night, I made out the shiny metal surface of a nail completely embedded in my rear tire. The tire seemed relatively full of air, but I knew it was unlikely that would continue to be the case as I traveled 500 miles on the treacherous road back to Fairbanks during the following two days.

I had packed a patch kit and spare tubes in my panniers but did not have room for the larger tools that would have been required to do a repair myself. Having made notes earlier about auto and truck mechanics in the area, I left messages with a couple of businesses telling them about my situation in the hope they might be able to help me the following morning.

It was hard to fall asleep that night as my mind swirled with questions about what to do with the bike the next day and I breathed in fumes from the fuel that had leaked from the spare gas canisters I had stowed in my over-heated room. I had been instructed not to open my window, due to the presence of bears in the area, so I willed myself to set aside my frustration over the broken thermostat and my concerns regarding the bike repairs, and focus on getting the rest I would need for the arduous return trip south. I also resolved to continue with my plan to take the tour bus to the Arctic Ocean in the morning. I knew it was unlikely I would ever have another opportunity to swim in the below-freezing waters.

Following a short night's slumber, I arranged for a local truck repair shop to look at my bike later in the morning, ate breakfast in the Deadhorse Camp cafeteria, and got on the tour bus along with Mike, Brad, and Hardy to ride through the oil fields and past the foraging reindeer to the ocean.

After we parked on the gritty, rock-strewn ground surrounding the silver-blue waters of the Arctic, the three of us disembarked to look at the crusty, partially ice-covered ocean shrouded in thick fog. Carrying towels to wrap ourselves in after our icy plunge, we crunched through the gravel in our boots, stopping to commemorate the occasion by taking pictures of our surroundings. At one point, Mike turned to me and smiled mischievously, shouting, "Jump!" Not sure why he asked but ready to do anything to celebrate such a memorable occasion, I leaped into the air, raising both fists and grinning in jubilation, my red emergency locator device swinging back and forth on the carabiner attached to my jacket. The shot Mike captured of that joyful moment with me in midair ended up being one of my all-time favorites and one I proudly display in my family photo wall at home.

Reaching the water's edge, I took off my motorcycle boots and socks, as well as my jeans and jacket, leaving just my dark gray underwear and the long white T-shirt loaned to me by the oil worker the night before. Although my bottom half was covered just as much as I would have been in a bikini, I felt a little self-conscious about my lack of swimwear and announced to the other tour guests nearby, "Don't worry, I'm wearing underwear under this." Mike, who had been standing close by ready to take pictures of me in the water with my phone, grinned and said enthusiastically, "It doesn't matter; we've seen it all already anyway," apparently alluding to the bathroom break mishap from the day before.

Initially mortified by his rather brazen comment, I laughed along with him, knowing that, although we had met just the night before, I could consider him a friend. I also knew that any embarrassment I might feel about the situation was irrelevant in the context of our remarkable achievement in making it to such a remote outpost.

I had decided that dipping my toes in the frigid water would not be sufficient to celebrate all that I had overcome to reach the Arctic. So, with a sense of determination, I pushed forward beyond the border of the chilly waters, gingerly placing my feet as carefully as possible on the gray, brown, and black rocks of all sizes and shapes littering the ocean floor. As I moved out farther, my legs and calves ached from exposure to the twenty-nine-degree waters, and the bottoms of my unprotected feet could feel the sharp bite of the jagged rocks beneath me. Taking a deep breath to firm my resolve, I lowered my entire body into the ocean, floating on my back with both arms outspread and only my nose and mouth remaining above the surface.

As I raised myself out of the icy waters and lifted my hands in victory, I felt a deep sense of peace and joy, knowing that whatever ended up happening next, I would carry this moment of triumph with me forever. I posed for a few more pictures, with Mike acting as photographer, to realize only later that the thin, wet, white T-shirt I was wearing did little to hide what was underneath!

It may not have been a bathing suit, but this long-sleeved white T-shirt loaned to me by an oil worker did the job, making it possible for me to fully submerge in the below-freezing waters of the Arctic.

After I changed back into my clothes on the bus along with the other women who had gotten wet, the rest of the group got on board to return to Deadhorse Camp. As we stepped off the vehicle, we were each handed an "Arctic Polar Bear Club" membership certificate from the tour organizers.

Back at camp, rain and mixed snow flurries started to fall, and the guys got on their bikes to head south in the frigid cold, while I gingerly rode my now-flat rear tire the short distance to ASRC Energy Services, a local business that repaired the tires of the massive trucks working the oil fields. Although no one there had ever fixed a motorcycle tire, two mechanics, TJ Bennett and Clint Davis, gamely removed my tire and tube, patched the rubber, and put the tube and tire back on the bike. Because the tire was still leaking a little air, I rode the bike

another thirty miles or so and then re-checked the pressure
back at the shop to make sure the patch would hold.

*Although TJ and Clint normally serviced the tires of the heavy semis
carrying supplies back and forth along the Haul Road, they both
gamely helped me repair my damaged tire with the tube patch kit I
had brought with me.*

At that point, I was very concerned about the condition of
the Haul Road, because it had been raining for several hours,
and the dirt road had turned to mud, something the seventy/
thirty tires on my bike were not equipped to handle, even
when in the best of shape. While TJ and Clint re-checked my
air pressure, I added an extra layer of clothing and took some
deep breaths, summoning up the courage to head down the
Haul Road in the freezing cold on the mud, with a patched-
up tire on my bike and two damaged panniers carrying my
essential supplies.

As I cinched up the multiple straps valiantly holding my
bags together, the bespectacled and bearded shop foreman,
Tom Saltmer, stopped by to say hello. Watching me tying the
pieces of my luggage to the side of my bike, he hooked his
thumbs in the sides of his mud-smeared dark blue overalls,

leaned back on his heels, and commented, "I wish you could speak to my men about the value of perseverance and determination in the face of difficult circumstances."

Thanks to the guys at ASRC Energy Serivces, I am eady to hit the road again.

His encouraging comment provided just the confidence boost I needed in that moment. Although I knew I would be facing an extraordinary challenge, I made the decision to attempt the passage south, knowing that I had limited time to return the bike to its owner and non-refundable lodging reservations along the way. Little did I know that at my weakest point later that day God would dramatically demonstrate his power and provision for me in a moment that would change my life and my perception of myself forever.

What had been a challenging ride in dirt and gravel over Atigun Pass on this day became almost impossible the next, after rain and snow flurries turned the surface into slick sludge.

CHAPTER 7

PLUCKED FROM THE MUDDY DEPTHS OF THE DALTON

Shortly after hitting the road, I was struck by the enormity of the job in front of me. The rain that had been falling for several hours had permeated the dirt and gravel surface, turning it into deep, slushy mud. As my adventure bike tires were designed primarily for pavement, they had no large knobs or deep grooves to dig into the sloppy mess and provide grip. As I gamely tried to find the best gear and speed for the bike, I felt my tires slip and slide underneath me, giving me the sensation of skating on ice in a pair of ill-fitted boots with broken laces.

Reaching a sixteen-mile section of road construction I had navigated the day before, I downed a large protein bar while waiting for the pilot car to come my way, knowing that I would need as much energy as possible for the task ahead. Although none of the other areas under repair on the Haul Road had any personnel managing traffic, this section of road apparently warranted some extra supervision. There were dozens of large, lumbering vehicles with enormous tires circling in the road, backing up to drop off loads, and then pulling forward to head in another direction. As is the custom in these cases, I was first in line, right behind the escort vehicle, with all the heavy semi-trucks traveling down the Dalton in a row after me.

As the pilot car flashed its lights and headed south with me following behind, I took a deep breath and sent up a prayer for my safety, not sure how to manage in such deep mud with so many large vehicles on all sides. I suspect the pilot car driver, a middle-aged woman with a head full of dark curly hair in a sludge-splattered vehicle, had never driven a motorcycle in such conditions, because she alternately sped up to over fifty-five miles an hour in the soupy surface and then slammed on her brakes with no warning. I tried to maintain enough distance to give myself room to stop but not so much space that the heavy semis behind me would try to pass, showering me with wet slush and potentially causing a collision.

My heart hammered in my chest as my bike swayed underneath me, slipping and sliding down the road with its handlebars shaking violently back and forth. The large ruts created by the heavy equipment ran in all directions on the road in front of me, making it impossible even to set a straight path for the bike in one of the four- to six-inch mucky grooves. I was exhausted from the constant danger and the ongoing spikes of adrenaline as the bike rocked back and forth, and I narrowly missed dumping it moment after moment with all the large semis bearing down on me from behind, their large, looming headlights filling up my rear-view mirrors. With no solid surface in sight, no pullouts of any kind, and all of the machinery around me, I didn't know how I could go on any longer. I was out of breath and did not think my heart could stand the onslaught of stress and the treacherous conditions much longer.

As I hit a particularly deep stretch of slop with grooves running sideways across the road in front of me and my bike shuddered violently, time slowed down as my mind acknowledged the possibility that death could be imminent. In the span of a fraction of a second, I asked myself what would hurt more: dumping the bike, getting run over by the semi behind me, or if I survived, trying to explain to the kindly owner of the rented bike how I had totaled his machine?

At that moment, I knew I could not go on. I lifted my hands off my handlebars and cried out to God, "I can't do this any longer!" Expecting to crash and bracing myself for the collision with the truck behind me, I was shocked to feel my bike being lifted out of the muddy rut, placed squarely back on the road, and set on a straight path moving forward, somehow seeming to gain purchase with the wet sludge underneath it. An unexpected sense of peace filled my body, and my heart rate lowered as I moved forward down the road.

Surprised to still be alive and not sure why I remained upright, I couldn't process in that moment what had just happened. I was confused by the fact that I had felt a crash was imminent and yet found myself still traveling in the right direction down the road. There was no logical explanation why I would have felt my bike rising out of the mire. Although the world around me continued as it had before, with construction vehicles beeping and backing up, the pilot car fishtailing down the road, and semis looming behind, I felt as if something in my existence had changed. I had a deep feeling of inner well-being, believing that God was somehow showing his care for me.

I shook my head to try to fling some of the slush off my helmet, gripped my handlebars, took a deep breath, and decided to focus on the road in front of me, grateful to be in one piece.

The warm welcome I received from this kind trio of fellow motorcycle adventurers had a life-changing impact.

CHAPTER 8

A PERSPECTIVE-CHANGING HOMECOMING

I continued to slip and slide down the road, making my way through the rest of the construction zone and then, not long afterward, heading up Atigun Pass. The temperature dropped, my fingers became numb, the rain turned to slush, and snow appeared on my left and right. Even though I had escaped the muddy ruts of the road construction, I was now faced with a new challenge as the still soupy road itself pitched and rolled in front of me, winding up and down and around the large, mountainous pass. Muck splattered all over me and my bike, and as I tried to wipe the sludge off my face shield, the grime all over my gloves transferred to my visor, making it difficult to see in front of me. As I slipped down a particularly steep section of road, my low fuel warning light came on. With absolutely no shoulders or even any flat sections of road to stop on, I continued, hoping my fuel would hold out until I could find a place to park the bike.

Right after rounding a corner on the pass, I spotted Hardy, one of my biker companions from Deadhorse, pulled over examining his bike on a small triangle of mud near the edge of the road. I was surprised to see him there, as he had headed south several hours before me. I would have loved to stop and say hello and make sure he was okay, but I didn't believe I could safely maneuver my bike over to him on such short notice. So, I waved as I passed, hoping there might be somewhere down the road we could meet up soon.

Soon afterward, my fuel warning light started blinking furiously, indicating that I was in imminent danger of running out of gas. Relieved to see a flat section of the road up ahead nestled between two steep mountain passes, I pulled my bike to a stop for the first time since I had waited for the pilot car at the beginning of the construction zone. I was relieved to have the opportunity to replace the fuel in my tank but concerned that I was a sitting target in the middle of the road. I struggled to get my muddy gloves off my numb hands as quickly as I could, then eagerly pulled a fuel bottle out of one of my pieced-together panniers but could not get the cap off at first with my muck-covered, frozen fingers. As I did my best to open the bottle, I wondered what would happen to me if a semi materialized over the hill behind me before I could get back on my bike.

As I was finally pouring gas into my tank, Hardy appeared in my rear-view mirror. We smiled in recognition, and he stopped briefly on the road next to me, explaining that the vibrations from the rough terrain had loosened several crucial nuts and bolts on his bike. He had patched his motorcycle together with bungie cords but needed to stop periodically to adjust the straps. We both commented on how difficult the day had been, and he encouraged me by translating a metaphor from his Indian heritage related to having accomplished the hardest part of a challenging task. Referencing the idea of trying to push a large elephant through a tiny hole, he said, "The elephant is out of the hole, and only the tail is left," trying to lift our spirits with the idea that the worst might be behind us.

As I looked ahead on the road, I could see a small sliver of blue sky a few miles ahead, and I nodded in agreement, visions of dry dirt in my head. It had been a tremendously hard day, but it looked like the potentially drier road up ahead might provide some much-needed relief. As Hardy continued south and I vigorously attempted to shove my grimy gloves back on my icy hands, I looked to my right and saw a sign posted on the edge of the road right next to me, "No stopping! Avalanche Zone!"

I focused on Hardy's encouraging words as I motored south the rest of that day, stopping again to put the remaining fuel from my bottles into my tank. I had made nonrefundable reservations for the evening in Wiseman, a mining community with a population of twelve, located three miles off the Haul Road, about halfway between Deadhorse and Fairbanks. Although the rooms there were half the price of those at nearby Coldfoot Camp, the small enclave of buildings had no gas, food, or other services and would require me to travel six additional miles before gassing up. With my fuel running low and me being exhausted from the challenges of the day, I threw money concerns aside and decided it was a better idea to go directly to Coldfoot, where I could fill up on both fuel and hot food and, hopefully, find a room for the night. I also knew that my three riding buddies from Deadhorse had planned to stay there, and I was hoping to reconnect with them.

With just a few miles left to go before Coldfoot, I was relieved to see Hardy up ahead. I honked my horn to get his attention and sped up to join him, hoping he would be willing to get me some fuel if I ran out of gas before arriving at the weather-worn collection of metal outbuildings.

There were two entrances into the camp, and the two of us ended up taking separate paths to the gravel and dirt parking lot. As I rounded the corner and spotted the sole gas pump in the dusty space, my eyes watered with tears of gratitude that I had survived the harrowing conditions of the day and had made it to the safety of the small outpost. Running on fumes, both literally and physically, I coasted directly up to the pump, lowered my kickstand, and gingerly dismounted from the bike.

Covered in caked-on mud from the trying road conditions earlier in the day, the bike and I were both glad to reach the safety of the gas pump at Coldfoot Camp.

Hardy had pulled up in front of the camp's dining building and had been met by both Mike and Brad, who were relaxing over some beers after their long ride earlier in the day. When I stopped my bike across the parking lot from them, Mike lifted his head to see me and yelled out, "Kathleen—you made it!"

In a move I will never forget, Mike spontaneously ran toward me with both arms outstretched, his huge grin bursting forth from above his neatly shaved silver goatee and below his mustache and ruddy red cheeks, with his kind eyes twinkling in the twilight and sandy hair tousled from being inside his helmet all day. Utterly relieved to be alive and so grateful to have such an enthusiastic welcome, I ran toward Mike with both arms raised and impulsively jumped up onto him, wrapping my legs around his tall torso and leaning my helmet-clad head against his neck, freely crying tears of joy and feeling the comfort of his warm embrace. Mike held me tight against his chest, swirled me around and around, and placed me back down on the ground, exclaiming, "Kathleen, you are the bravest woman I have ever met!" Brad and Hardy swarmed around us, joining Mike in hugging me and slapping me on the back and pronouncing, "Yes, Kathleen, you are so brave. So very brave."

Back on the ground with the dust swirling around my mud-crusted boots and the encouraging words of the three men echoing in my ears, I took in the surreal moment and looked around me, aware that in that instant my life as I had known it had forever changed. Even in the chaos and emotion of the minute, I could see that there was a sizeable shift in my perception of myself. No longer was I the woman afraid to ride up her own driveway, terrified of living alone, and praying to God to be taken in the night to escape the horrors of my abusive marriage. I was Kathleen the Brave!

In that moment, it was as if any remnants of the depressed, shame-filled, hopeless woman of the past had finally been completely removed from my body and soul, falling away like the dried-up, caked mud tumbling off my boots. Although I had been learning to see myself as more of a person of value and strength for the last several years, the moving, life-changing divine encounter earlier in the day, combined with the enthusiastic homecoming celebration of my fellow bikers and adventurers, had helped me to fully grasp the breadth and depth of the new person I had become.

No longer mired in shame and doubt or paralyzed by fear, I could see the full extent of God's grace and provision for me, favor that extended to me even in the muddy ruts of the Dalton and through the kindness of others, even in the remote outreaches of Alaska.

Although I had known about God's grace on an intellectual level for many years, for most of my life I was still stuck in thinking that I had somehow had to earn this favor. If I was a strong enough student, a kind enough friend, an obedient enough daughter, a loving enough mother, a successful enough teacher, and a devoted enough wife, then God would bless me. I had strived so valiantly for decades to be the best at whatever I did—high school valedictorian, dedicated parent, reliable friend, hard-working employee, and faithful marriage partner. But when I discovered that my second husband was not who he said he was and, in fact, had betrayed me at the deepest levels in so many unexpected ways, it was as if the wheels on the school bus of my life had fallen off. I struggled to make sense of how things could have gone so horribly wrong.

Filled with pain by all the lies in my marriage, I had found it difficult to be a completely present mother, had a hard time fully connecting with my students, and found myself too exhausted and worn down to reach out to most of my friends. Devastated by what I had discovered about my husband's behaviors behind my back, I fell back on what had always driven me through difficulties in the past—working harder at fixing the problem. I used money from a refinance of my home to pay for counseling and treatment for my husband, joined a support group for wives of sex addicts, and saw my own therapist for guidance and help.

However, no matter what I did, the problems in our marriage were not resolved. As lie after lie surfaced, it became harder for me to continue, always wondering when the next shoe would drop. My husband's hair-trigger temper, manifested in screaming, swearing, and physical violence, continued to take a toll on me, even when I was suffering through chemo and radiation. I soldiered on, sure that if I got a second divorce it would be an indicator that I had failed, that I was not good enough to be used by God or to deserve any favor.

What I didn't understand at the time was that God's grace was not something I could ever earn, that it was a gift offered freely and required me only to accept it (*footnote 1*), whether I was "successful" or not. Although it had not been possible for me to fix the problems within my marriage, that didn't mean that God cared for me any less, that I was any less deserving of experiencing the fullness and abundance of God's compassion.

After my divorce, I had begun to learn that God did not need me to be successful to bless me, but that, in fact, his grace for me was more abundant when I was at my weakest. (*footnote 2*) As I acknowledged my own shortcomings and limitations, focused more on my faith and less on my performance, and trusted God to provide for me, I began to see levels of confidence, joy, and hope in myself I had never thought possible.

In retrospect, I think my experience with God in the muddy ruts of the Dalton that day had such an impact on me because it was such a powerful, life-changing, miraculous physical manifestation of God's power, grace, and provision in a time of an impossibly difficult and potentially deadly plight. When I didn't think I could go on any longer, cried out to Him, and lifted my hands from the handlebars, he lifted me up out of the rut and put my safely back on the road, calming my racing heart and setting me on the path toward safety and shelter.

When I then arrived at Coldfoot Camp and was so heartily greeted by my fellow adventure riders, it was as if their love and compassion toward me accentuated and confirmed what I had been learning spiritually. I was clearly not fully prepared for the Dalton Highway, having only a few years of limited riding experience under my belt and traveling alone on a

1. *Ephesians 2:8–9, The Holy Bible:*

"For it is by grace you have been saved, through faith—and this is not from yourselves, it is the gift of God—not by works, so that no one can boast." (NIV)

2. *2 Corinthians 12:9 The Holy Bible:*

[The LORD] said to me, "My grace is sufficient for you, for my power is made perfect in weakness." (NIV)

rented bike without proper tires or secure storage. I had left Prudhoe Bay with a patched-up tube and tied-together bags after hours of rain had turned the roads into a thick sludge difficult to manage under the best of circumstances. Yet rather than criticize me for my lack of training or proper equipment, my newfound friends warmly welcomed me, lifted me off the ground, and embraced me, showering me with love and encouragement—a perfect picture of God's own affirming love.

When the dust cleared in that parking lot at Coldfoot Camp, I felt fully conscious of the new person I had become— more secure in God's love for me, more aware of the extent of his grace and power in my life, and more confident than ever that he would provide for me in times of hardship.

Although I knew I would prepare differently if I were to travel the Dalton again, I was grateful that I had persevered, overcome all odds, and succeeded in reaching the northernmost tip of the United States. With about 250 miles of mostly dry dirt road left to get to Fairbanks the following day, I knew the most challenging part of my Alaskan journey was behind me. However, as I continued south, I understood that I would be doing it as a different woman than the one who had left for Alaska less than two weeks earlier.

When Adventure Baby was being loaded up to travel to the shipyard in Maine for its journey to Iceland, I had no idea the medical news I would receive just three-and-a-half weeks later would force me to consider cancelling the voyage.

CHAPTER 9

FACING FEAR FROM A POSITION OF POWER

It was less than a year later when Dr. Burton called and told me I had four potentially life-threatening tumors in my brain. In that moment, facing down shocking and unexpected news, I also had a surreal sense of peace, believing even during that phone conversation that God would be with me as I bravely faced whatever difficulties lay ahead.

The information itself felt terrifying, but I knew my response to it did not need to be driven by fear. Over the last few years, as I had faced obstacles both on and off the road, I had learned that while I would invariably encounter a variety of anxiety-provoking situations in my life, it was up to me how I chose to react to those events. I had gradually become able to respond to fear from a position of power, rather than powerlessness. Instead of focusing on all the reasons why I might not be able to overcome a challenge, I started to ask myself how I could respond in a productive manner and what

I would do if fear were not my first thought. Then I would ask God for the courage to take the first step in the right direction.

Learning to move forward constructively, rather than being paralyzed by anxiety, was a skill I had had to re-learn after the years of feeling helpless and trapped in my abusive marriage. Having strived so valiantly to save the marriage but failing so miserably, it was tempting to think of myself as someone incapable of successfully overcoming obstacles.

My perception of myself began to improve after a pivotal conversation with a neighbor shortly after my divorce, when I decided to face my fears of being alone and head off on a solo eight-week cross-country motorcycle trip. I had been yearning to travel long distances by bike over the summer, as I had done the previous five years with my husband, but did not feel capable of doing it by myself, as I had never even taken a one-night motorcycle trip on my own! Despite my longing to be on the road, I was fixating on all the reasons why such a trip was not possible—my bike was not equipped for luggage, I did not know how to deal with mechanical difficulties, and I was afraid of how I would feel about spending so many days alone.

I had tried to find a riding partner who could accompany me on a summer adventure but could not locate anyone who had the same days off or who was willing to travel just months after the 2020 outbreak of the COVID pandemic. I was also desperately missing my son, as he lived across the country in Washington, DC, and we had been separated for several months, due to concerns with long-distance airplane travel with the pandemic raging.

I shared my dilemma with my friend and neighbor, Roger Bufford, a tall, lanky college professor and professional counselor who tends to make stunningly astute observations with a minimum of words. Amid my lamenting, Roger rather abruptly announced, "Kathleen, I know exactly what you need to do." Hopeful he might have some great advice for me, I drew in a deep breath and held it as he continued,

"I think you need to take your bike to Washington, DC, to see your son." Letting out my breath after hearing such a grand pronouncement, my knee-jerk reaction was to ask, "But how am I supposed to do that alone?" His matter-of-fact response was exactly what I needed to hear: "You have three months to figure that out."

In that moment, my love for my son, my passion for riding, and my trust in the judgement of my friend and neighbor allowed me to shift my thinking from all the reasons I couldn't make a solo summer trip to what steps I would need to take to make it happen. I began investigating the types of luggage that could be attached to my motorcycle and how to have it installed, plotting different routes with which to travel east, and setting up safety precautions for while I was on the road. I began to more fully understand something very important: that facing a fear didn't have to be accomplished all at once, but conquered one step at a time.

Traveling solo over 100,000 miles since that timely conversation with Roger, but before the call from Dr. Burton telling me about my brain tumors, I had learned that as I successfully faced a variety of rather daunting obstacles, one after the other, the victories along the way gave me the courage I needed to continue to respond to fear in a helpful manner. Now I could move in the right direction from a perspective of strength.

Although nothing could have fully prepared me for the devastating medical news I then received from Dr. Burton, the lessons I had learned had created in me an awareness of the value of moving forward during a time of difficulty, instead of giving up before the battle even started. So I picked up a pen and posed my question: "What are our next steps?"

Dr. Burton explained that I needed to get both an MRI and a PET Scan, ideally as soon as possible. Although it was almost four o'clock Friday afternoon when I got off the call with him, and both imaging scheduling offices soon would be closing for the weekend, I was determined to do something constructive. I called the MRI department as I walked out to my car with my school bag over my shoulder, listening to their hold music and texting my four o'clock tutoring client to let them know I would not be able to keep our scheduled time.

Sobbing with emotion over the stunning information as I crossed the street to the staff parking lot, I evaluated my next steps. I felt a palpable sense of sadness to be facing such daunting news not long after recovering from throat cancer and so soon before my planned summer trip. I also grieved for my adult children, wondering how they would respond to my medical condition and imagining how difficult it might be for them if I were to pass years before they thought they would lose me. Although I was resolved to face this trying circumstance from a position of power, my heart hurt for Ethan, Elliot, and Eleanor and what they might encounter on the road ahead.

Should I tell my children the news right away or wait until I had more information? Did I think I could work with my five o'clock tutoring client or the four others I had scheduled that evening? What on earth was I supposed to do with the Honda CB500X adventure bike I had already purchased and freighted across the country to be shipped to Iceland? Would I be able to use the nonrefundable plane ticket I had booked to Reykjavik for just two-and-a-half weeks later?

Although I had no idea if I would still be able to take the trip, I knew I wasn't going down without a fight. Rather than cancel plans because I might not be able to go, I vowed to do everything possible to address the brain tumors in my head and keep my summer options open, not to mention prolonging my life as long as possible. So instead of collapsing in a crying mess at my desk or in my car, I continued to move forward, making my way toward home, and preparing a mental to-do list, confident that I could be strong in the days ahead.

After a half-hour on hold, the scheduler came on the line, only to tell me there were no regular openings in the next few weeks and that the supervisor who would need to approve an earlier appointment would not be back until Monday. We talked briefly, and I was able to explain how challenging my situation was, both because of the urgency of the medical issue and because of the immediate and costly travel plans I already had in place. The PET scan department was now already closed, and I decided I had done everything I could for the evening.

As I contemplated how to spend the next several hours, as well as the following few days, I felt a palpable sense of urgency to get more information about the tumors in my head, knowing that a brain cancer diagnosis could potentially mean my remaining life span would be measured in months rather than years. Finding out whether the tumors were cancerous and what the recommended treatment plan was would allow me to make the most of the life I had left. It would also help me to determine whether the European motorcycle trip I had saved for all year was still feasible. I was determined to move forward with the planning for the trip, still reasoning that I would rather do that and have to call it off than to quit trying to make it happen because it might end up needing to be cancelled.

At the time I received the devastating phone call, my adventure bike had already been trucked across the country to Portland, Maine, and was being prepped for loading on an Eimskip ship headed to Iceland. I emailed Jonathan Blatchford in customer service, who informed me that the vessel my bike was booked on would leave the following Wednesday afternoon. Once it left its port in Portland, Maine, I would be committed to paying the $1,600 shipping fee to get it to Reykjavik, not to mention a similar return fare if I needed it shipped back. If I sent the bike and ended up not being able to go on my trip, I would have to pay thousands of dollars more to get it back to Portland, Oregon. However, if I didn't send the bike and ended up being able to go, I could end up in Iceland without a motorcycle.

The next five days were a whirlwind of activity as I called my children and contacted the rest of my family with the news, cancelled plans for my weekend ride, worked with doctors and imaging departments at OHSU to schedule the needed PET scan and MRIs, and arranged for subs and colleagues to cover my classes at the high school. I was able to get three MRIs done on Saturday, the day after I received the devastating news, when another patient cancelled their appointment and the scheduler called me back to tell me about the opening. The brain tumor board met on Monday to review my images. Dr. Hans Kim, who had helped me in my cancer battle several years before, lobbied on my behalf with the nuclear medicine department to get my PET scan done by Tuesday, the very next day. Dr. Timur Mitin, the head of my current throat cancer team, agreed to meet with me the morning after that, the same day I had to make the Wednesday call to Eimskip to tell them whether to ship my bike.

The possibility of brain cancer would have been frightening under any circumstances. But to face it after already having battled throat cancer just three years earlier and to get the news just two-and-a-half weeks before leaving on a sixty-day European motorcycle adventure was downright daunting. I found myself starting to worry about the future, asking myself questions like "Will I ever see my grandchildren?" and "How would my kids handle facing the rest of their adult lives without their mother?"

And of course, "Will I ever get to go on another long-distance motorcycle trip?"

Since there was no way to know the answers to those questions immediately, I decided to concentrate on taking productive steps to get the information I needed. I also started focusing on the good things that could come from my situation, whether I was diagnosed with brain cancer or not. With a potentially life-threatening medical condition on the table, my perception of what was truly important seemed to become much clearer than it had been just a few days before.

It meant the world to me that my mom, pictured here with me at Oregon Health and Sciences University, and other family members and friends stood by my side and encouraged me throughout the process of diagnosing my brain tumors.

CHAPTER 10

BLESSINGS AMONG DIFFICULTIES

Given the startling news I had received, concerns about logistics related to work or household maintenance immediately faded into the background and were replaced with thoughts about how to connect more lovingly with my closest friends and family. My children, all of whom are young adults, showed remarkable strength and compassion, letting me know in small and big ways how much they cared. Not sure what the ultimate outcome of my diagnosis would be, it became more important than ever to convey to those closest to me how much I valued and cared for them.

My daughter mailed me a touching letter titled "Sending you a bear hug," accompanied with a hand-sketched picture of the two of us. She drew herself leaning out of a castle tower window with her long, blonde hair cascading down her side, yelling "Mom, help!" and depicting me rushing up the hill to her rescue on my motorcycle, shouting, "I'm coming, my beautiful daughter!" (my favorite endearment for her). She added on the side, "What I imagine anytime I call you for advice." I treasured her sentiment, as it was so gratifying to know that she could see the depth of my devotion to her. Although I will not be in her life forever under any circumstances, it is heartening to understand that whenever I leave her, it will be with her knowing she has been deeply loved.

This treasured note from my daughter filled my heart with joy as it reassured me that she understood the depth and breadth of my love for her.

My older son, Ethan, had two of my favorite matcha milk boba teas delivered to the house, exactly to specification—thirty percent ice, zero percent sweetness, and lychee jelly layered on the bottom of the fresh milk concoction.

More importantly, he initiated a heartfelt conversation with me laying to rest an unresolved issue between the two of us. Three-and-a-half years earlier, while heavily medicated and in a great deal of pain from the radiation and chemotherapy treatments I was receiving, I had lost control and said some harsh and inappropriate things to him. While we had continued to connect on a variety of levels, spend time together, and express positive sentiments to one another, I knew that there was still distance caused by my outburst. I had been concerned for him, worrying that if I were to pass unexpectedly, it might be harder for him to manage if we had unfinished business.

Although I desperately hoped to close the gap between us, I did not know when that might occur. So, when Ethan called me the day after I got the news, I assumed he was checking in on me and my health. When he brought up the issue from the past, my heart started palpitating and my hands trembled at the welcome prospect that we might be able to resolve it. With a catch in his voice and a depth of emotion to his words, he conveyed his love for me, his gratitude for the things I had done for him, and the fact that he forgave me for the words I had expressed before. With tears running down my cheeks, I told him how much I loved him and how much his phone call meant to me.

After the call with my son, I reflected that whatever my prognosis ended up being, I would be forever grateful for the peace achieved between Ethan and me. It was a tangible reminder that God has a future and a hope for me, whatever my circumstances might be. I could make the most of each day, regardless of how many more days I had left.

The medical news I had received also opened a door for me and my own mother to draw closer to each other. As soon as my mom, a retired physician, heard the news, she offered to come with me to my medical appointments. I was grateful for the offer of her assistance and insight but concerned that she would be spending a lot of time waiting for my procedures to be completed. She reassured me, "I'm your mom—of course I want to help take care of you." It was such a blessing to feel her support in such a tangible way during such a challenging situation.

My best friend since high school, Michelle Martin, also came to my side, driving several hours from her home in Bend, Oregon, to be with me after my MRI and go to church with me the next morning. Michelle hugged me, held my hand, prayed for me, and cried with me, comforting me with her presence and her words of wisdom. When my mind started drifting toward all the potential hurdles I might face in the future, Michelle gently placed her hand on my arm and brought me back to the present with the words, "Let's just find a way to get you through today."

Although I was working on taking one day at a time and feeling grateful for the good that was coming out of my situation, I would be lying if I said I wasn't hoping I would still be able to take my sixty-day European motorcycle vacation. I had spent many months working out the logistics for such an enormous adventure—buying a new motorcycle, customizing it to fit my small stature, outfitting it for a long-distance trip, purchasing riding gear appropriate for extreme temperatures, figuring out how to get both myself and the bike to Iceland, and making ferry reservations to get to the Faroe Islands and Denmark after that. To make the trip financially feasible, I had been tutoring after school, typically working for six hours a night on work nights and up to ten hours on Sunday.

As I rode up the elevator of the Kohler Pavilion at OHSU on Wednesday, June 7, along with my mom for my appointment with Dr. Burton and Dr. Mitin in the radiation oncology department, I knew I had just hours to call the shipping company to tell them whether to take my bike to Iceland. Although the neurosurgeon who would make the final call about whether I could go on my trip would not be able to meet with me until a few days before my scheduled flight two weeks later, I was hopeful that Dr. Mitin would provide enough information based on the test results so far for me to make an educated decision about the bike.

During my appointment, Dr. Mitin explained that the tumor board thought the growths were probably benign, that he wanted to do an additional MRI to get more information, and that it was likely the neurosurgeon, Dr. Aclan Dogan, would want to monitor me for a while before making any decisions regarding surgery or radiation treatments. Dr. Mitin said it was impossible to predict the next steps, but that if it was him, he would send the motorcycle.

Elated about the potentially good news, my mom and I rode the elevator down to my car in the parking garage and pulled over when we exited the structure so I could call Jonathan at Eimskip. "Ship the bike," I declared with a hitch in my voice and a welling up of tears in my eyes, overcome with emotion over the magnitude of the decision, the stress of the last several days, and the prospect the trip still might be on.

The next ten days were especially challenging, as I waited for the final go-ahead from the neurosurgeon while simultaneously preparing as if I would be going to Reykjavik. I arranged for one neighbor child to pick up my mail and another to do the yardwork while I was gone, paid my bills for the month in advance, started packing my motorcycle luggage, began researching places to stay in Iceland the first week, cleaned the house, and submitted final grades for my students. I also put the finishing touches on plans to attend both of my twins' college graduations in two separate states in the four days between my appointment with Dr. Dogan and my scheduled flight to Iceland.

More determined than ever to live every moment to the fullest, I celebrated my younger son's college graduation with him just a few days after meeting with my neurosurgeon to discuss my prognosis.

CHAPTER 11

IT'S ABOUT THE RIDE, NOT THE DESTINATION

During the wait for my Friday, June 16, neurosurgery appointment, it was difficult not to focus on all the uncertainties in my future. I love to organize and would have preferred to have been packing and re-packing all of the gear for my trip, plotting out riding routes in Iceland, and looking up great local restaurants in Europe instead of traveling to and from the hospital waiting for more news from the doctors. With so many issues about my health not resolved, I knew that making a final decision about how to spend my summer might not be easy.

Well-meaning friends were concerned about the risks of my leaving for a summer trip, even if Dr. Dogan gave the go-ahead. They asked me what would happen if my double vision deteriorated and I was unable to see with my prescription goggles. Some were afraid that my brain tumors might grow over the summer, and I would develop debilitating symptoms while in a foreign country. One neighbor was concerned about recent reports of petty theft in Europe and felt I should consider cancelling my trip because of robberies that might occur during my travels. My children also very reasonably made it clear that they did not want me to leave if doing so would in any way compromise my medical care or potentially shorten my life expectancy.

Even under the best of circumstances, I knew it was unlikely I would ever be able to completely rule out a brain cancer diagnosis. The doctors had explained to me that images of that area of the body cannot conclusively rule out cancer and a biopsy of my brain likely would not be recommended because of the possible damage that could be caused by such a procedure. It was rather unnerving to realize that I potentially had four little ticking time bombs in my head that could go off at any time.

I started wrestling with thoughts about how I wanted to spend the rest of my life, given the uncertain nature of my medical condition. One thing I knew for sure was that I didn't want to view life through a lens of fear, avoiding living to the fullest because of all the potential problems that could occur if I did.

As a natural planner by nature, one of the aspects of life on the road that appealed to me so much was the way in which it had taught me to live completely in the moment. My typical workday during the school year includes helping students before school between eight o'clock and 8:30AM, teaching classes during the morning and afternoon, proctoring tests at lunch, racing home at 3:30 to make a salad for dinner, then tutoring clients every hour on the hour between four o'clock and ten or eleven o'clock in the evening. Although I absolutely loved helping my high school students understand complicated math concepts and teaching my tutoring clients to become more proficient and comfortable with the materials given to them by their teachers, almost every minute of my day is scheduled by necessity.

Because I am so passionate about my work and care so much about my clients, my energy during the day is focused on meeting the needs of others—determining how to convey a concept clearly, motivate a student on the brink of giving up, manage a class full of freshmen to maximize their productivity, create equitable tests, and respond to parents in a clear and helpful manner. I strive to be patient, loving, kind, and firm, regardless of circumstances.

Shortly after donning my first motorcycle jacket and heading down the street on the back of my second husband's motorcycle in 2014, I realized that being on a bike gave me a level of freedom and excitement I didn't normally experience in my day-to-day interactions with others. As we swooped around corners, leaning into the wind and barreling down the road, I learned that riding a bike allowed me to experience the world around me with more breadth and depth and appreciation than ever before.

With only a helmet between me and the outdoors, I was able to interact with the environment using all five of my senses, feeling more alive than ever. As I rode past the ocean, I could taste the salt in the air on my tongue, smell the seaweed, hear the waves, feel the sun on my back, and see the rocky outcroppings.

I also learned to appreciate every instant as it came, because my route for the day after that could not be predicted ahead of time. While it was often practical to have a general itinerary in mind, plans often needed to be changed due to unforeseen weather conditions, road construction, or even driver fatigue. The only sight I was sure to see during the ride was the one in front of me at that second, making whatever I was looking at on a moment-by-moment basis much more precious. Although I could never guarantee reaching my destination for the day, I could enjoy every minute of the ride with all my senses, a sentiment I have captured on one of my biking T-shirts: "It's About the Ride, Not the Destination." (*footnote*)

Once I got my own endorsement in 2019, I understood even more fully that complete situational awareness on a bike was not just a benefit but a necessity. It was one thing to get behind the wheel of an automobile while slightly tired or distracted, but another concern altogether when riding on two wheels, directing a 700-pound, 73.7 horsepower machine with no seatbelt or protective cage. A colleague at work summed it up astutely when he said to me while walking into work one day, "Kathleen, I know why you have to be living in the moment while you are riding your motorcycle!" "Why is that?" I responded. "Because otherwise you're dead!" he exclaimed with a huge grin, a slap on his legs punctuating his remarks. Although his comment was said in jest, we both understood that being aware of my environment while on my bike was no joke.

As I spent more time on my motorcycle, I began to realize that the lessons I had learned about being fully present while on it could help me while I was off the road as well. I had wasted so much of my life regretting the past or worrying about the future, and I realized I had sometimes missed out on the one thing I could control—my own actions in the moment.

For the longest time in my abusive marriage, I had wallowed in the shame of my poor choices, sure that there would be no hope for me after a second divorce. I had also felt anger and sadness about the ways my husband's actions had been so hurtful. However, after finally getting the courage to leave and beginning to pull myself back together, I began to understand that mistakes and other difficulties can shape us but do not have to define us. A fixation on events of the past can hinder us from taking healthy steps toward healing in the present.

As I began to focus on what I had to be grateful for and to look for opportunities to build my life anew, I felt less encumbered by the events of the past and more able to appreciate my current circumstances. I also began to place more value on my interactions with others, being willing to set aside a task or plan to fully and completely engage in a meaningful conversation with a loved one.

On one occasion while I was preparing an inspirational speech about being more fully present, my phone rang, and I could see that it was my daughter calling. My initial reaction was, "I'm too busy working on a speech—this isn't a good time to talk." Then I caught myself and realized I was missing an opportunity to live out exactly what I was writing about. I picked up the phone, put my feet up on my desk, leaned back in my chair, and focused on connecting with Eleanor.

Although time with my only daughter has always been precious, my motorcycle travels have allowed me to better understand how to be more fully present with her, whether on the phone or while visiting her in San Diego.

So, when the morning of June 16 arrived, and my mom and I headed to OHSU for my neurosurgery appointment with Dr. Dogan, I had decided that although it was unlikely my tumors would ever go away, I could choose to change my perception of them. Rather than thinking of the growths in my brain as potential future threats to my life, I determined to view them as timely gifts. I had already begun to learn the importance of being present in the moment, but the tumors had brought into a much sharper perspective the transient nature of every day, the extent to which we all truly cannot know what tomorrow will bring. While I couldn't know whether the tumors would end up shortening my life, I could decide to live the days I had left more fully. I was more resolute than ever to seize life by the horns, riding it for all it was worth. If Dr. Dogan gave me the go-ahead to leave on my summer trip, I would head out intending to savor every bit of it.

I took an instant liking to Dr. Dogan, beginning with the intake questionnaire his office manager gave me asking, "What are your top three goals for today's appointment?" "That's easy," I thought, "asking about the feasibility of my summer trip, next steps, and life expectancy." Dr. Dogan walked into the exam room in his white lab coat and with a genial smile, his dark brown eyes and closely trimmed peppered hair conveyed warmth and professionalism.

He immediately got down to business, letting me know that the tumors appeared to be benign and stable for now and that he wanted to wait three months to do more imaging before making any decisions about radiation or surgery. My heart soared at this news, and I immediately asked, "Is there any reason why I should remain in the country for the next two months—would leaving alter any recommended treatments or plans for my health care?"

Aware of my travel plans from messages I had left with his scheduler, he responded by letting me know I was free to go. I spontaneously leapt out of my chair and gave him a hug, my heart pounding at the significance of his words and a feeling of relief and gratitude washing over me, realizing that the trip of a lifetime was indeed on! He continued, telling me that there was a possibility that the tumors would remain stable forever and not adversely affect my lifespan. We would continue to monitor them every few months and make treatment plans based on the information we received at that time.

After the appointment with Dr. Dogan, my mom and I drove back to my house, where I kicked into high gear, trying to put my household affairs in order before leaving the next morning for my daughter's college graduation in Southern California and her twin brother's university graduation in Oregon three days after that. I would return to my house just the evening before my Wednesday, June 21, flight to Iceland, with a few short hours to finish packing. Working under such a short timetable to put the finishing touches on a logistically involved trip was daunting, but my only real emotions were gratitude for the opportunity to take the trip and joy over the possibility I might live for decades more.

The graduation ceremonies over the next few days would have been memorable and touching under any circumstances, but as I basked in the good news from Dr. Dogan, I was practically giddy with happiness about the opportunity to spend time with my children during such a momentous part of their lives. I treasured every hug and every minute, reflecting on how accomplished they all were and how grateful I was to hopefully have many more years with them.

Arriving back home the night before my flight to Reykjavík, I realized that I couldn't fit everything I needed into the travel bags I had set aside for the trip. With shops closed for the night but determined to pull everything together, I managed to locate a dry bag used for another trip and repurposed it for my Iceland adventure, packing some additional straps and making a mental note to use some of my time on the plane to think through options for securely attaching the bag to the bike once I arrived in Iceland.

In the morning, as I donned my tall adventure boots, put on my new, thick-layered textile jacket, and prepared for my good friend Grant Myers to pick me and my bags up for the ride to the airport, the events of the prior two weeks seemed almost surreal. I had already been through so much trauma and turmoil over the previous several years and had not expected to face such challenging circumstances again so soon. But I couldn't help noticing how much I had changed as a person since the last time I had dealt with an ominous medical diagnosis. In some ways, my trip to Iceland represented a tangible celebration of the new life I had created from the lessons I had learned through facing the trials and overcoming the obstacles of my past.

When Grant pulled up at the departure level of the airport outside the Iceland Air ticket counter, I asked him to take a picture of me in front of the airport's revolving doors, standing with my luggage cart filled to the brim and my thumb raised high. It seemed fitting that this fellow biker, a former US Air Force staff sergeant and retired transportation manager, would be the friend to send me off on such an epic adventure. Grant, a tall, soft-spoken, mechanically gifted man with a white mustache, twinkling eyes, and generous smile, had graciously helped me to transport the motorcycle through the snow when I purchased it a few months earlier, assisted in assembling the luggage I would be using on the bike that summer, and provided me with mechanical support by phone on my previous three summer trips.

Bursting with joy outside the airport doors shortly before taking off along with all my gear for Iceland, I gave the thumbs up to Grant, grateful to be heading off on such a lifetime adventure after the uncertainty of the previous few weeks.

After checking my bags at the ticket counter and getting permission to carry my helmet onboard, I passed through security, boarded my flight, and sat down in my seat, relieved and joyful to have finished all my preparations for the trip to Reykjavik. My eyes welled with tears of gratitude for the opportunity to embark on such a significant journey to Iceland, the Faroe Islands, and much of the rest of Europe.

As the plane taxied down the runway and the roar of the airplane's jet engines filled my ears, I reflected on how happy I was that I had not given up hope for the trip when I received the difficult news just two-and-a-half weeks before. I was so thankful I had been able to respond to the challenge in a proactive manner and to reframe the troubling news in a way that helped me to see my circumstances in a positive light. My heart was full of joy, anticipating the adventures, challenges, and even obstacles I might face in the upcoming weeks. I was more determined than ever to savor each moment, appreciate every mile, drink in all the vistas, and value each personal interaction along the way. How might my heightened awareness of the temporary nature of life on earth help me to learn to more fully appreciate the days I had left?

The massive wide, sweeping vistas and enormous natural wonders of Iceland captured my heart from the very first day.

CHAPTER 12

FAITH-BUILDING DAY IN REYKJAVIK

Seven-and-a-half hours later, as I peered out the airplane window while my plane touched down at the Keflavik International Airport, I was immediately struck by the starkness and vastness of the horizon laid out in front of me. Gone were the rolling hills of Portland, Oregon, and present was the far-reaching brown and green grass-covered tundra accentuated by numerous gray and blue fjords that outlined the dozens of peninsulas along the coastline.

As I stepped off the plane, I was startled by a blast of chilly wind, incongruous to me at the end of June. What, I wondered, was the temperature like in the winter? Relieved to be reunited with my motorcycle luggage shortly thereafter, I rode a bus to Reykjavik and then took a taxi to the Eimskip shipping warehouse that was storing my Honda, a bike I had affectionately nicknamed my "Adventure Baby."

After a month of separation, I was delighted to see Adventure Baby in the back of the shipping yard—dusty, a little low in the tires, and with a loose rear-view mirror but ready for action. After carefully loading his gear to keep the weight down low and a quick stop at a local motorcycle shop to get him in tip top shape, we headed north.

I was lucky to catch this eruption at the Great Geysir just a couple of hours after leaving Reykjavik.

The road north to Gullfoss, one of Iceland's most treasured waterfalls, was chock full of one calendar-worthy photo after another—thick-maned horses prancing in the fields, wide lush green meadows surrounded by colorful purple wildflowers, and snow-capped mountains in the distance.

As I headed north, I stopped in Thingvellir National Park to take a short hike to a beautiful waterfall cascading off dark brown rocks and sending a fine mist to brighten the moss covered stones around it. A few miles down the road, I also pulled over to catch a glimpse of the Great Geysir, apparently the geyser after which all others are named. I was fortunate to walk up to it right as it was erupting and managed to catch the tail end of the burst of steam on my camera.

The most breathtaking moment of the day was my first glimpse of Gullfoss, an enormous, wide, multi-tiered, cascading waterfall that stretched off into the distance, sending sheets of mist and rain in all directions on top of delighted spectators. The massive planes of white water pounding the pools at the base of this natural wonder stood in stark contrast to the dark, rocky cliffs behind them and the bright, green-covered earth stretching out on both sides. I took a picture of myself nestled in the clefts of the waterfall, the plumes of mist surrounding me on all sides as I breathed in the cold Icelandic air.

I had been on a long flight with little sleep the night before and had ridden many hours on the road so far that day, so I was a little nervous I would be too tired to ride to my youth hostel back in Reykjavik for the night. However, once the chilly rain started coming down and I had to open my visor to keep my goggles from completely fogging over, the biting raindrops pelting me as I sped along did a great job of keeping me alert!

After checking into my lodging, eating a hot bowl of soup, and spending some quiet time writing and reflecting while the cold Icelandic wind howled around me, I began to organize my gear for the following day's journey.

Finding my expensive prescription motorcycle goggles' case empty, I scanned my eyes around the room, searching for the safety eyewear as my heart started racing. After weeks of struggling to see the previous year, I had finally been diagnosed with a severe case of double vision in January, a condition that might have been caused by the then not-yet-identified brain tumors. It had taken several months to find a doctor able to design a prescription to help me see normally, and the goggles I had were specially made at a lab in Florida and took weeks to obtain. I had purchased a backup pair of the several-hundred-dollar item to take with me to Europe, knowing that I would be unable to ride without the specialty eyewear if the first pair were lost or damaged. However, the prospect of losing one of my two pairs on the first day of my trip was terrifying. After searching every crevice of the room several times, I had to acknowledge that the goggles were gone.

Retracing my steps that day, I realized I had set the goggles down on the counter when I had checked into the youth hostel. While speaking with the clerk about the fact that the $165 a night "budget" rooms had no soap, shampoo, or towels to use in the communal showers, a guest had suggested I follow another visitor to a lost and found bin where I could pick out some personal hygiene supplies to use during my stay. When I returned to the register shortly afterwards, the goggles were no longer there, but in my haste, I had failed to recognize the fact.

I raced downstairs to speak with the night clerk and to check the bottom floor of the hostel for my goggles but could not find them anywhere. She suggested I contact the manager at ten o'clock the next morning, as he could review the security tapes and hopefully identify a suspect to question. Returning to my room, I felt defeated and demoralized. I was disappointed in myself for being so careless so early in my trip and felt vulnerable without a backup pair of goggles. The severity of my medical condition and my fatigue from the long flight and busy riding day hit me like a train, and I began to wonder if I had the skills necessary for such an arduous summer trip.

Fortunately, I called my friend Kathy Nesper, a devout, brilliant, and compassionate mother of three adult children, and she talked some sense into me. A good friend for the previous twenty-seven years, she had had a front row seat to observing how God had helped me through the trials of raising young children, losing two marriage partners through divorce, and surviving cancer. Her matter-of-fact approach to life's difficulties, easy smile, beautiful long, silver hair, and generous heart complemented her razor-sharp mind and years of wisdom. As a member of my safety team on each of my previous three summer solo trips, she had also witnessed firsthand how God had provided for me during mechanical break downs, severe weather, and challenging road conditions.

On one particularly notable occasion, I had been struggling with an issue with the starter on my Harley while visiting my nephew in St. Louis, Missouri. Unable to turn on my bike before breakfast with Tom and his fiancée, I had tried replacing the battery in the fob, jump-starting the bike, and entering the PIN code as a back-up mechanism, all without success. After repeated tries with the PIN, I was finally able to get the engine started to drive to breakfast but after the meal experienced the same problem all over again.

It was a Sunday, and there were no open Harley dealerships in the area, so I decided to head south to Lambert's Café in Sikeston for lunch and use the two-hour drive to come up with a plan. While on the bike, I prayed for wisdom, having no idea why I was experiencing mechanical difficulties or to whom I should turn.

While gassing up at a Mobil station in Sikeston next door to the café, a young man with salt-and-pepper colored facial hair and wearing a black doo-rag and a Darth-Vadar T-shirt walked up to me and said, "Aren't you that lady that's traveling around the US doing book signings in each corner?" I briefly engaged with him but then explained that I was distracted because of the mechanical issue and described the problem. The jovial fellow, Matt "Cheezy" Parks, smiled at me, said he was part of a company called MRRC (Motorcycle Rescue Recovery Company), and pointed to his trailer outfitted with a wheel chock that was parked right in front of me in the gas station! I am convinced that this good Samaritan was an answer to my prayers. Wow!

Matt and I had pushed my dead-again bike over to the side of the gas station and walked next door to the café. We talked over lunch and gallon-sized containers of unsweetened iced tea and came up with a plan to trailer the bike over 300 miles to Rogers, Arkansas, where I knew the service people at a Harley dealership that would be open the following morning. After arriving the next day and determining that the antenna to my starter was defective, I was able to locate a replacement part a few hours away in Tulsa and have the bike repaired and back on the road by three o'clock that afternoon.

Matt, a good Samaritan at the Mobil Station in Sikeston, Missouri, had been parked at the pump right in front of me just when I needed him most.

It wasn't only during my trips that I had seen the full extent of God's provision for me. Just a few months before arriving in Iceland, I had received the news that, due to some paperwork that had fallen through the cracks as I transitioned between accountants, I would be owing $10,000 in taxes that spring. As a schoolteacher and single mother of three, two of whom I was still supporting through college, this was devastating news. Although I worked multiple jobs to provide for my family, I knew that I could not continue to pay toward college for two, make my monthly mortgage payments, and go on a summer motorcycle journey.

I prayed about it that night and decided that I would need to be willing to give up my summer adventure. Maintaining a home for my family and keeping my financial promises to my children was more important to me than going on another trip. Although I knew the decision was the right one, it was a difficult pill to swallow, because the time on my bike between school years was the highlight of the year. Over the timespan since my first solo journey and after publishing my first book, I had become an inspirational speaker and gained a following, sharing with others how my time on the road had helped me to gain confidence, joy, and hope after surviving throat cancer and my second divorce. It wasn't just the adventure I was concerned about missing but also the opportunity to build more of a platform for my speaking engagements and encouraging messages.

The next morning, I saw an alert on Facebook and decided to call a friend I had made through the app to wish him a happy birthday. I had become personally acquainted with this kind gentleman the year before after he had read my book and reached out to me via Facebook Messenger to share his own life story. A former US Marine and fellow motorcyclist, he had been exposed to Agent Orange in Vietnam and was suffering from health complications because of his time overseas. Shortly after our conversation began on the day of his birthday, he asked me, "Kathleen, where are you planning on going this summer?" At first hesitant to share but deciding to be forthright, I explained that I wasn't sure I was going on a trip after all, due to the unexpected financial news the day before.

His next words shook me, "God told me to ask you where you were headed this summer. He also told me to help you get there." The timing and nature of his comments, so soon after I had decided to give up my trip, sent a wave of hope and joy through me. There was no earthly explanation I could come up with for him to make such a statement right after my prayers the night before.

It turned out that this generous retired Marine was receiving substantial monthly disability checks because of his wartime injuries. Since he no longer could go on cross-country trips himself and was supportive of the positive message I was sharing with others, he hoped to become a sponsor for me, making it possible for me to continue going on journeys and telling my story. Over the next few months, he provided significant financial support while I also worked three jobs to garner the resources to purchase and outfit an adventure bike and send it to Iceland.

Now, hunkered down and demoralized in my hostel room in Reykjavik that night in June, Kathy reminded me of how many ways God had provided for me on these and other previous occasions and admonished, "Don't you think that if God wants you to take this trip you're going to be able to do it?" Her words comforted me, bringing instant confidence that everything would work out. I was able to fall asleep that night knowing that I would either find my goggles in the morning or proceed on my trip without them.

Quickly showering and getting dressed the next morning, I arrived at the desk promptly at ten o'clock to ask the clerk if I could speak with the manager about my lost prescription eyewear. Instead of calling him over, she asked what my goggles looked like, then gave me a huge smile, saying, "We found them!" The night manager had discovered them on top of a garbage can in the middle of the night but had not wanted to wake me up to return them to me. Apparently, the thief had put them on, realized they produced double vision of everything, and decided to discard them.

Buoyed by the recovery of my essential travel eyewear, I loaded up the bike and headed southeast along the Ring Road, grateful to be embarking on my counterclockwise loop around Iceland. My weather app showed a mere thirty- to forty-percent chance of rain later in the afternoon, and I was hopeful for an easy day on the bike appreciating the natural wonders of the island. Little did I know I would face some of the harshest riding conditions I had ever experienced.

With glistening white ice, ash-streaked and pock-marked walls, and blue-tinged highlights, the Katla Ice Caves near Vik provided breathtaking views to those tourists willing to navigate across the rickety wooden pathways suspended over an icy river.

CHAPTER 13

SOMETIMES A PIVOT IS PRUDENT

Within a few miles of Reykjavik, I realized the day's ride was going to be much less about enjoying the scenery and much more about surviving the wind and cold. As I worked my way toward my lodging for the night in Vik, enormous gusts from the ocean swept across the flatlands and pounded and buffeted the bike and me, slewing rain sideways and wailing in my ear. My bike tipped precariously, my left handlebar leaning toward the ground and the right reaching up into the sky. My heart hammered in my chest as I realized my options were limited. There were no rest stops, large buildings, or pullouts where I could seek shelter. I didn't feel able to stop the bike on the road, believing that the strong wind would slam me against the ground if I did not keep forward momentum.

The frigid temperatures outside exacerbated the problem, as it was impossible to ride with my visor closed because my warm breath immediately fogged up the surface, obscuring my view of the road in front of me. My unprotected face became red and puffy with pain as the ice-cold rain pelted it.

Despite the extraordinarily harsh conditions, I managed to pull over twice that day, both times at enormous, strikingly beautiful waterfalls along the route. The first, Seljalandsfoss, is considered one of the top attractions in Iceland because of its stunning, sixty-meter undulating drop from sheer cliffs covered with bright moss and framed by a carpet of vivid green grass at the base.

Hiking behind the Seljalandsfoss waterfall, I could see the far-reaching green tundra beyond, framed by brown and gray rocky cliffs and sheer white walls.

As I tried to recover from the challenges of the ride, I focused my attention on taking in every aspect of the waterfall's breathtaking majesty, watching the sheets of water tumbling in waves and hitting the frothy white pool at its base. Wanting to experience the natural beauty with all my senses, I decided to hike through a cave behind the feature, breathing in the cold, damp air and hearing the echo of the water beating down as I gazed out at the green horizon through the curtain-like stream falling off the cliff. Coming back around to the front of the waterfall, I stood on a rock near its base, raising my hands in victory as the water from above rained down on my damp hair and already wet, jacket-clad body.

As I was already soaking wet from riding through rain most of the day, I decided to take in all of the glorious Seljanlandsfoss, placing myself within reach of the cascading streams of water.

Just a few miles down the road, the Skogafoss Waterfall also beckoned, another famous Icelandic attraction considered especially beautiful from above. After climbing over 500 stairs with my biking gear on, I was more than happy to rest at the top, watching the water cascade over the rocky cliff and pound the rocks jutting out below, spewing water everywhere.

Reaching my boarding house in Vik that night, I realized I needed to reevaluate my riding strategy for Iceland. My gear would help protect most of my body from the rain and cold, but I was concerned about the level of risk posed by riding in the almost gale-force winds. After I expressed my concerns to the manager of the establishment, he introduced me to the Icelandic Meteorological Website, an online resource that charts the temperature, precipitation, and wind in six-hour increments throughout the day, several days in a row. The wind levels are shown in a spectrum of color, with light green representing little to no wind, followed by light blue, dark teal, and then purple for up to twenty-two meters per second (fifty miles per hour).

The website forecast for the following day showed purple levels of wind on my way north after noon, a condition the manager explained would not be safe, even for motorists traveling in a car. After experiencing the death-defying gusts earlier in the day, I did not need to have it explained twice. Not normally a morning person, I woke up at the crack of dawn the following day, ate a quick breakfast, and rapidly loaded up the bike before hitting the road.

Although I was only able to stop for a few minutes in the driving cold and rain to admire the Jokulsarlon Glacier Lagoon, I was nevertheless transfixed by the white and blue chunks of rocky ice floating in the frigid waters.

Although the riding conditions that day were challenging, they were manageable, and I was able to appreciate the white- and blue-tinged fingers of the Skaftafell National Park outlet glaciers, flowing down the mountains and toward the road like rivers frozen in time. I stopped briefly to admire the breathtaking views of the Jokulsarlon Glacier Lagoon, a gray- blue body of water formed by melting glaciers and filled with bright multi-colored icebergs. The heaping piles of ice floating on the water reminded me of a raspberry slushie, with streaks of bright blue swirled with white, all in a frosty mound.

The following morning, I continued north, following the fjords on the eastern side of the island along the frigid, wind-swept shores of the coastline and then heading inland to Egilsstadir and west toward Dettifoss Falls. Along the way, I passed purple wildflowers and long, green grass blowing in the wind, little creeks and streams rippling and swaying around rocks and boulders, and majestic waterfalls cascading down mountains in the distance. The scenery was so vast and magnificent, yet so sparsely populated that I felt as if I had been transported back in time to the Jurassic Age.

Shortly after leaving Egilsstadir, the landscape became flat and barren on both sides of the road, creating an opportunity for the strong island winds to build up momentum across the dusty landscape. Grass was replaced with blackened, scorched earth for miles in either direction. Large plumes of dirt filled the air, making it almost impossible to see the road. As the gusts around me picked up speed, I realized that the moderate wind forecast the night before had unexpectedly turned deadly, and I struggled to keep the bike upright as I continued west.

Conditions worsened when I turned north for Dettifoss Falls, as the stormy weather was now blowing the bike sideways and more wind-blown soil filled the air. I gamely proceeded, turning through a wide curve in a cloud of dust and then descending blind into dirt-filled darkness, wondering aloud to myself, "Is this what hell is like?"

After several more exhausting miles along the access road, with my bike buffeting wildly back and forth every time a large tour bus passed, I managed to park in the visitors' parking lot at Dettifoss. From there I hiked to the stunning body of water and drank in the beauty of Europe's second most powerful waterfall, spanning 330 feet and dropping 144 feet. Its location between moss covered rocks and steep cliffs jutting up to the sky created a marked contrast with the barren landscape surrounding it.

Back at the bike, I ate a small snack for energy for the rest of my ride, doing my best to ignore the crunching of grit in my mouth, blown there by the relentless wind. I was relieved to make it to my lodging for the night, stopping briefly to admire the Namafjall Geothermal area with boiling mud surrounded by multi-colored sulfur crystals.

The following day I treated myself to a whale watching tour in the Eyjafjordur, a body of water considered one of the best in the world for spotting the massive mammals, as the volcanic fissures in the bottom of the ocean emit heat that attracts the zooplankton and krill they like to eat. The weather was unusually sunny and mild, and I was delighted to get up-close views of twelve humpback whales and one minke whale as they surfaced, spouted, flipped their tails, and sang songs for me and the rest of my small tour group. When one of the enormous creatures came particularly close to the boat and crested the water right in front of me, I was terrified and elated at the same time, shrieking with joy while pictures of the movie *Jaws* flashed through my head.

With the sun on my back, blue water surrounding the boat, snow-capped mountains on each side of me, and beautiful creatures leaping through the air, I reflected on how grateful I was to have such an extraordinary opportunity to experience one of the most beautiful locations on earth. The tour provided a welcome respite from the harsh riding conditions of the prior several days before I hit the road for my lodging in Blonduos that night.

My trip the following day was one of my favorite segments of the summer journey. I traveled hundreds of miles by pavement and then dirt past fjords, snow-capped mountains, rich mud flats, and lush green grass to Skafavik, the northwesternmost point of Iceland, just 200 miles away from Greenland. The tip of the Peninsula was so barren, yet inviting, with thick green grass on the hill leading down to the water and a cove nestled by cliffs on both sides and the ocean's waters gently lapping at its base.

A highlight of the trip, I raised my hands in victory to have made it to the far northwestern hamlet of Skafavik, just 200 miles from Greenland and accessible only by dirt road.

Having stopped earlier in Isafjordur to pick up a replacement fuse for one that had blown in my electric gear the day before, I returned to the same town later that evening to enjoy a rich, hearty, all-you-can-eat buffet in a nondescript building that looked like an abandoned barn. The Tjoruhusid Restaurant was warm and inviting and offered fish of all shapes and sizes—cod cheeks, halibut, Atlantic wolffish, and more cooked in a variety of amazing sauces—garlic and onion, hoisin, sweet chili, and some kind of mushroom cream.

As I savored every bite of my meal, I deliberated about which route to take in making my way south the following day. Both options were risky from a safety standpoint. One required traveling on mud through rain and fog to a ferry that would take me directly to my lodging in Stykkisholmur for the night. The other would require hundreds of miles of travel in what the meteorological website was categorizing as the highest possible levels of wind. Although my bike was well equipped with fifty/fifty tires more than capable of handling most dirt roads, the incessant rain would turn the most direct route into a soupy mess, reminiscent of the Dalton I had ridden in Alaska.

Deciding that I was better off on murky mud than in gale force winds, I elected to ride through the mountains of the Vatnsfjordur Nature Preserve the next day, leaving early the morning, hopefully minimizing the extent to which the unpaved roads were soaked with rain. After riding through two mountain tunnels that provided a brief respite from the rain and fog, the road transitioned from asphalt to mud. As I bumped and jostled down the wet dirt path, I focused on avoiding potholes, loose gravel, thick pockets of sludge, and cars coming the other direction on the narrow way. It was almost impossible to see in the thick fog, and several cars had moved to the side of the road to wait out the weather. Unable to find a safe place to pull over, I regulated my breath and tried to keep the bike in fourth gear and moving forward, appreciating the progress I was making and trying hard not to think about how many miles I might have left.

A few miles before the ferry landing in Brjanslaekur, the road turned to pavement again, and the ocean appeared in front of me. Although the wind was strong so close to the water, my heart soared, and I laughed with happiness to be on asphalt again and so close to my destination. I found refuge in a small café near a little church at the top of a gravel road. There I celebrated surviving the ride by enjoying hot tea and warm strawberry rhubarb pie topped with whipped cream before heading by ferry across the Breidafjordur body of water to my lodging for the night.

The next day I explored the Vesturland Peninsula, taking in multi-tiered waterfalls cascading down jagged rocky cliffs, black sand beaches framed by rippling white and gray waves, and even a volcanic crater formed by the outward explosion of rocks several thousand years ago. Riding in the rain, fog, and cold, I passed green fields with grazing sheep and craggy, snow-capped mountains towering over little villages as I completed a full loop around the Ring Road of Iceland, reaching Reykjavik for my second time.

After spending the night in the country's capital, I headed toward Vik once again, stopping this time at the Hveragerdi Geothermal Park, a 100-kilometer geothermal area used to heat cold ground water and generate electricity. Strolling alongside rivulets of steaming sulfur water, I read about the area's history and then paid to boil an egg for lunch by placing it in a mesh net on the end of a long wooden pole and dipping it into the hot water in a grated hole below me. Fortified by the time of rest and the warm food inside me, I headed east on the bike to the Reynisfjara Black Sand Beach near Vik.

Voted one of the top ten non-tropical beaches in the world by *National Geographic* in 1991, this area features large basalt stacks, roaring Atlantic waves, and breathtaking vistas of black sand framed by the sea. It was relaxing and inspiring to gaze out at the ocean, crunch my feet in the crisp, dark grit as I walked along the shoreline, and look up at the paragliders swooping and swirling their way down from the tall, green-covered cliffs jutting out to sea.

I spent the following morning exploring the Katla Ice Caves nearby, traveling along with a tour guide through tunnels of ash and ice with crampons on my motorcycle boots, enjoying the sparkling white, blue, and gray walls glistening with water. As I navigated over a series of rickety walkways suspended high in the air above the rapidly moving glacial stream below, I grasped the loose strings of rope hung between the icy walls streaked with volcanic ash while the frigid water roared below me and a waterfall cascaded down in front of me. I was grateful for the guide's assistance traversing the unsteady walkways, as my fear of heights and his warnings about the deadly consequences of a fall into the icy rivers had caused me to hesitate. However, I had not come that far to back down in a watery cave in Iceland, and I gripped his outstretched hands with determination while carefully inching across the unstable walkways. The stunning, shimmering, blue-tinted views of pockmarked ice along the way made every step worthwhile.

So many shades of gray and black! The massive silvery basalt stacks, crunchy dark and rocky sand, and roaring waves make the Reynisfjara Black Sand Beach one of the most beautiful in the world.

Returning to Vik with the tour guide in our mud-covered, battered four-by-four Jeep, I checked the meteorological website on my phone while our leader tried to navigate by downshifting, as the vehicle had abruptly lost its braking ability. Concerns about mechanical failures with the Jeep faded from my mind as I noted the dark, purple-coded wind forecast for the following three days on my route north. I had originally hoped to spend several days leisurely traveling along the coastline from Vik to Egilsstader, arriving there the day before my ferry, in the neighboring town of Seydisfjordur, left for Denmark.

Having experienced the island's death-defying winds several other times earlier that week and knowing I could not afford to miss my ferry in four days, I realized it was time for me to pivot. While it is true that my travels over the previous three years had taught me a lot about overcoming obstacles and facing fear, I had also learned that not all challenges are meant to be conquered.

There are times when a difficult situation cannot be changed but, instead, needs to be embraced. The recent news I had received about the tumors in my brain was a vivid reminder of that fact. Since I could not safely remove the growths, the healthiest response for me had been to reframe them as a timely gift, reminding me of the preciousness of each day.

In other cases, I had found it wisest to avoid a risky situation altogether, either for my own safety or out of respect for loved ones concerned about me, a lesson that had been brought forcefully home to me the previous winter.

Instead of traveling to Iceland, my initial summer plan for 2023 had been to ride my motorcycle south through Central and Southern America to Peru. I was enchanted by the idea of walking through the ruins of Machu Pichu, as well as completing my earlier travel on the Pan-American Highway. It is a mostly paved road that stretches all the way from Prudhoe Bay in Alaska south to Ushuaia, Argentina, with a small break in coverage at the Darien Gap in the Isthmus of Panama. I hoped to store my bike in Peru or a neighboring country and then travel later to the southernmost tip of the continent.

My children had told me over the Christmas holidays that they were worried about me traveling through so many areas rife with political tensions and fighting drug cartels. I had acknowledged their fears but assured them that my preparations were extensive enough to mitigate many of the challenges of the trip. Indeed, I had spent dozens of hours over several months interviewing fellow female motorcyclists who had safely managed the journey, contacting hosts along the way, researching recommended roads, developing a plan to navigate around the Darien Gap, determining what paperwork would be required at each border, procuring maps, picking a bike for the trip, and starting Spanish lessons.

At the end of January, amid planning my trip, my daughter texted me, asking to schedule a Facetime call over the weekend to discuss her concerns with my summer travel plans. I intended to listen to her apprehensions, empathize with her feelings, and explain to her kindly that I intended to go south anyway. I hoped she would understand that after years of being paralyzed by fear, I was eager to take on the hardships associated with such a once-in-a-lifetime adventure.

But when Eleanor and I connected via Facetime, I could see the extensive strain on her flushed, red face and hear the depth of emotion in her words as she kindly, respectfully, and lovingly explained her concerns. She told me that if I traveled south, her fears for my safety would impact her ability to live her own life to the fullest, that every day while I was on the road she would be wondering about my health and well-being. She also pointed out that the US State Department had travel advisory warnings in place for many of the destinations I had in mind, urging travelers to avoid those locations.

As I listened to her kind and reasoned approach to the problem, my heart swelled with love for my child. I was so proud of her for taking the initiative to reach out to me so respectfully with her thoughts and so grateful that she cared enough about me to have such a difficult conversation. Not wanting to make such an important decision on the spot, I thanked her for sharing and told her I would seriously consider her remarks and get back to her within a day or two.

Deep in the pit of my stomach, I knew that I could not proceed with my summer plans after a conversation like that with my child. As my only daughter, Eleanor has always held a special place in my heart. From the moment I first saw her after her birth and noticed her beautiful, slender fingers and endearing blue eyes, I have felt a fierce sense of love and protection toward her. With her long blond hair, tall stature, and breathtaking smile, she is stunningly beautiful. The generosity of her heart is even more striking.

As a youngster, she had always been caring and kind toward others. When she was a toddler and I ran a daycare in my home, she would regularly give our guests her own toys to keep, understanding that she would not be getting them back. Once, in the second grade, she saved up her allowance for three months to buy a stuffed animal sleeping bag for her best friend, leaving it on her front porch and running away after ringing the bell so the friend would not feel too indebted to her.

Raising three children as a single mom was not easy, but my love for all three made it possible for me to do whatever it took to provide for them to the best of my ability. Although my resources were often limited, I always made their well-being a priority—doing in-home daycare so I could be home with them during their early years, working several jobs, helping them with homework, hand-picking teachers most suitable for them, taking them on hiking and camping adventures, offering a listening ear, and assuring them that I would always love them.

I realized after talking with my daughter that it would be selfish of me to continue with my plans to travel through Central and South America. I couldn't in good conscience do something that would be so hurtful to her, regardless of how much I had hoped to make the journey. So, less than twenty-four hours after our Facetime conversation, I told her I was changing my travel arrangements. Even though I had spent months planning for a trip that I now knew I would not be taking, I also felt a sense of peace about my decision. Her grateful and loving response to my news confirmed that I had done the right thing.

I quickly kicked into high gear to come up with a new plan for summer, this time first looking at the State Department travel advisory site to determine possible alternative options around the world without significant travel warnings. I also reached out to several friends who had traveled by bike extensively to get their suggestions for other trips. The breakthrough came when a fellow rider, Gary Medin, responded to a Facebook comment I had made, describing his trip to Iceland and the Faroe Islands the summer before. Gary, a tall, enthusiastic, mostly retired realtor from Minnesota with a big smile, ruddy cheeks, and thick white hair, is an avid motorcycle adventurer, having traveled extensively in both the US and Europe, taking stunning pictures of his stops and the people he has met along the way.

Over the next several months, with Gary's helpful advice and extensive additional research, I was able to pull together the basic plan for Iceland and much of Europe, procure a bike appropriate for the trip, make arrangements to have it shipped to the island, reserve a spot on the ferry to Denmark, and choose some additional destinations. These included North Cape, Norway, the northernmost point in Europe that can be accessed by car, and Switzerland, a country I think of a second home because of my many visits to my grandmother there while I was growing up.

I had been extremely disappointed to give up my dream of traveling to Ushuaia in Argentina. However, after making what I knew to be the right decision, I discovered that changing my plans had not resulted in a loss. I had gained a priceless sense of well-being, knowing that I was respecting my children's wishes and tangibly demonstrating my love and compassion for them. The "alternative" plans I had made to travel to Europe had turned out to be more exciting and promising than I ever could have hoped for.

I had learned an important lesson—facing fears doesn't always mean overcoming the obstacle. Sometimes the most powerful response to a challenging situation is to pivot, willing to head in an entirely different direction.

So, as I bumped and jostled down the dirt road in the ice cave tour company's defective Jeep and heading back to Vik, I made the decision to avoid the three days of gale force winds entirely. Instead of taking the following several days to head over 350 miles to Egilsstadir, I would attempt to go the entire distance that day while the winds were moderate, leaving in the early afternoon and arriving before midnight. Because of how far north the location was, it would remain light out most of the night, making it possible for me to travel a third of the way around Iceland before the strong winds started the following morning. Once in Egillsstadir, I would hunker down and wait out the wind, heading out on smaller day trips when the gusts abated.

Although I ended up traveling a third of the way around Iceland in one day, I was happy I still made time to stop and take in some of the amazing views along the way from Vik to Egillsstadir.

The four nights I spent at the cozy and inviting Tehusid Hostel in Egilsstadir ended up being one of the highlights of my trip. I was able to travel to the tiny town of

Borgarfjardarhofn to visit a local puffin colony clustered on the rocky cliffs near the marina there, ride to the small coastal village of Vopnafjordur to see the fjord and snow-capped mountains surrounding it, walk to a local geothermal bath to relax in the hot waters and get one of the best massages of my life, and enjoy the delicious homemade soups offered by the hostel.

These cute little guys were a delight to watch on a short day ride from the hostel during a break in the wind.

In a fortuitous turn of events, I also discovered that the hostel's young cook, Wictor Stankowiak, was a budding photographer willing to do an extensive on-location photo shoot of me and Adventure Baby for a fraction of the price I would have paid back home, in order to get more experience and more material for his portfolio. During my stay at the hostel, we discussed goals for the session, possible locations to shoot from, and how we might set up the shots, eventually deciding to take pictures in the neighboring town of Seydisfjordur the afternoon before my ferry left for Denmark.

Wiktor ended up far exceeding my expectations, finding rustic and picturesque locations for the shoot, suggesting a variety of creative ways for me to pose, and enthusiastically standing up on bridge railings, lying on the muddy ground, and running circles around me to get the best angles with the correct lenses. With his boundless energy, larger-than-life-sized smile, cameras slung around his neck, and sandy brown hair flying in the wind, it was easy for me to be cheerful even after spending hours posing in the frigid temperatures with almost no layers on for warmth. Looking back on that day's wonderful experience, I was so grateful that my change of plans earlier in the week had made it possible for me to meet Wiktor and participate in a once-in-a-lifetime photo opportunity in Iceland.

Wiktor went to great lengths to provide a great photo shoot, from scouting out locations to suggesting poses and even lying in the mud to get this shot.

Traveling along the upper portion of the hump in the middle of this oil-slicked, one-lane road with two-way traffic and no lights was one of the most dangerous feats I have ever undertaken on a bike, causing me to reevaluate my plans for subsequent rides in the Faroe Islands.

CHAPTER 14

RIDE YOUR OWN RIDE

I had been looking forward to the following morning's Smyril Ferry Line ride to the Faroe Islands for months, both because the amenities on the eighteen-hour voyage across the northern Atlantic Ocean were so reasonably priced and because of the uniqueness and beauty of the destination itself. The Faroes, located between Iceland and Denmark, are a collection of eighteen volcanic, windswept Islands with jagged rocky cliffs connected by a variety of sub-sea tunnels. I was gleefully anticipating exploring the waterfalls, lakes, and hiking trails, as well as traveling under the sea by bike between land masses.

The voyage across the ocean turned out to be more eventful than I had hoped when I came down with a stomach bug, threw up in a garbage can in the ship's foyer while asking about anti-nausea medicine, and accidentally set off the fire alarm from the excessive steam in my room while taking a long shower trying to recover.

Rather than conversing over snacks with other world travelers in any of the ship's delightful eateries, as I had originally hoped, I collapsed on my bed in my cabin and slept for several hours before the ship docked in the capital city of Torshavn around two o'clock in the morning. Getting off the ferry with my bike was not easy, as I was weak from the illness and had trouble standing up and needed help carrying my bags down to the bike storage area. But after loading everything up on Adventure Baby, I managed to pilot the bike down the steel ramps and out into the parking lot at the terminal. Making my way to my Airbnb, I rested for a few hours and felt well enough to go on a ride to explore the islands late that morning.

My destination the first day was the tiny village of Vidareidi, a picturesque little enclave located in the far northeastern section of the archipelago. Following the coastline on Highway 10, I descended below the ocean's surface to find one of the most unique traffic patterns I had ever encountered—a roundabout under the sea where motorists could turn off to one of three different destinations, Streymoy Island or the western or eastern side of Eysturoy Island.

Chortling with glee as I found myself turning east under the water, I noticed that the tunnel itself was brightly illuminated in vivid blue and green colors, mimicking the appearance of the Northern Lights for which the islands are famous.

Exiting the tunnel, I continued along Highway 10 in the rain, taking in the views through the dense fog of the choppy ocean waters to my left, sheep grazing on the grasslands, waterfalls cascading down the moss-covered volcanic rocks, sheer rugged cliffs, grass-covered thatched huts, and little villages nestled in the fjords along the shoreline.

After traveling through another reasonably well-lit undersea tunnel that joins the islands of Eysturoy and Bordoy, I was unprepared for what I encountered right before arriving at my destination for the day. Entering a tunnel through the mountains just south of Vidareidi, I was stunned to find that this damp, primitive, one-lane passageway roughly hewn out of the rocks had no lights and no established traffic pattern to direct traffic coming both directions.

Even more concerning, the pavement itself was not flat but rather a narrow hump, with a raised middle portion of the single lane and sharply slanted sides leading down to loose rocks with no shoulder area whatsoever. The center of the road was covered with numerous oil spots, and my bike fishtailed wildly while I strived to keep it upright on the narrow middle section and avoid crashing on the gravel on either side of me.

I could see almost nothing, since my bike light did not illuminate most of the dark tunnel and the air was so wet that my goggles and shield fogged over. It was nearly impossible to keep the slipping bike from falling while taking my hand off the handlebars to wipe off my goggles.

I was grateful to make it safely out of the old passageway and enjoyed stopping at the church in Vidareidi to gaze out at the ocean, admire the cliffs jutting out to sea, and breathe in the fresh ocean air. Knowing that I had no alternative, I headed south through the same tunnel to head back to my lodging for the evening.

With only one more full day left on the Faroes and hoping to avoid encountering another hair-raising experience like the one in the tunnel, I put some extra thought that night into where I wanted to travel the following morning and afternoon.

I realized it was my responsibility to thoroughly research my riding options, not only to determine whether the route itself was a safe one but also with my personal preferences in mind. The same well-meaning biker who had given me the tip to ride to Vidareidi but did not mention the safety issues with the older tunnel on the way there had also recommended that I take a trip the next day to another small coastal town along older, more primitive roads.

Although I was interested in the destination he had suggested, I had learned early in my riding career that it is important for motorcyclists to "ride their own ride," an expression conveying the importance of making deliberate decisions as an individual regarding appropriate safety measures and routes, regardless of what a fellow biker might decide to do. For instance, while riding with another motorcyclist, a biker should make their own determination regarding what speeds to travel around corners and along straightaways, when to stop for rest or food, and how to operate their machine. The importance of this principle is significant, since bikers are much more likely to die in an accident because they do not have the safety features of a car such as a seatbelt, air bag, or protective cage.

So, instead of following the tip from my fellow biker, the following day I elected instead to travel to the island of Vagar to hike to Lake Sorvagsvatn, a large, stunning, sparkling blue body of water perched between two cliffs on the ocean's shore, giving it the illusion of floating above the sea. Although the weather forecast was again for rain and fog, I reasoned that even with less-than-optimal weather I would still be able to enjoy the physical exercise. The route there would also allow me to travel along newer, paved roads and through tunnels that were brightly lit and well paved.

As I chugged up one mountain pass and down another in the fog the next morning, I admired the sheep grazing on the sides of the road, resplendent in their black, brown, white, and tan long, wooly fur, and kept my speed below twenty-five miles an hour to avoid hitting any of the creatures leisurely ambling out into the road.

After first passing through a mountain tunnel and then an undersea one and descending further down the hillside, the fog miraculously lifted. With the sun shining for the first time in days, I felt as if a whole new world had opened before me. I could see little villages of vibrantly painted homes nestled on the hills along the water, vivid green grass blowing in the wind, and colorful wildflowers dancing back and forth under the bright blue and white cloud-specked sky.

With temperatures at fifty-five degrees and the warm sun beating down on me, I pulled over to take off my electric jacket and put on my summer gloves for the first time on this adventure. I was thrilled to be warm and would have stripped down to shorts and a tank top to dance in the street if I had had them with me.

After passing the town of Midvagur and turning near the church, I found the starting point for the hike, leaving my biking gear at the pay station there and donning my hiking shoes and tank bag turned fanny pack filled with water and a picnic lunch.

Deliriously happy with my decision to hike these trails on the island of Vagar, I soaked in the sun, gazed out at the ocean views, and skipped along the pathway singing songs from The Sound of Music *in my head.*

Grinning from ear to ear, I skipped down the narrow dirt path through the meadows, feeling like Julie Andrews as she twirled her arms and ran through the hills singing with joy in *The Sound of Music*, one of my favorite childhood movies. Stepping over tufts of brown, white, and black sheep wool, I decided to collect a few wisps to send to my children and support crew back home.

Transfixed by the brown, gray, and dirty white fur of these island sheep blowing in the wind, I decided to pluck some tufts of wool from the grass around me to send home as mementoes to my loved ones.

The hiking trail traversed a broad plateau between the lake and the cliffs near the ocean, meandering through meadows, streams, and gravel beds on its way to an amazing viewpoint of both the ocean and lake, with the latter appearing to be suspended in midair. I marveled at the views in all directions, with rocky outcroppings highlighted by the deep blue sky and frothy ocean waters, topped by the vast stretches of green grassy heathlands with grazing sheep.

Giddy with happiness, I created a 360-degree video of me and my surroundings to send to my daughter, my wide, toothy grin, exuberant voice, and heartfelt words conveying a level of joy I had never dreamt possible just a few years earlier.

I settled down on the grassy knoll for a picnic lunch, reveling in the feel of the sun on my back, the wind in my face, and the extraordinary views on all sides of me. I took a moment to contemplate how grateful I was that I had followed my heart to this magical location for the day.

Located on top of the cliffs directly above the ocean, Lake Sorvagsvatn's sparkling blue waters appear to be floating above the sea, drawing spectators from around the world to take in this captivating sight.

Delighted with my experience on Vagar, I returned to the island the following day before my ferry ride to visit the Mulafossur Waterfall on the northwestern tip of the land mass near the small town of Gasadalur. As I hiked along the cliffs there, I took in the beautifully cascading body of water plunging down to the ocean below, the foraging puffins with large orange beaks strutting along the sides of the rocky outcroppings, and the narrow mountain roads traversing back and forth across the lush green foothills before disappearing in the tunnels beyond.

On my way back to the island of Stremoy, I parked my bike on the side of the road and walked down a little path to a black sand beach, where I sat on a large rock by the shoreline and dug my toes into the gritty surface, savoring my last moments in the Faroes before boarding the ship for Denmark later that night.

As I rode to the Smyril Ferry Terminal in Torshavn, I considered how privileged I was to have experienced so many of the wonders of Iceland and the Faroe Islands, both breathtaking in their grandeur, majesty, and fierceness. I also reflected that the riding conditions I had faced over the previous twenty days had been some of my most challenging ever. Was it just me, I wondered, or did other bikers feel the same way about the unique difficulties of riding in these remote regions?

It didn't take long for my question to be answered. As I pulled up to the motorcycle loading area in the ferry parking lot, I was greeted with a friendly smile by Bernard, a tall, burly, sandy-haired biker with a dusty jacket and muddy boots whom I had briefly met in Seydisfjordur when loading up my bike on the ferry in Iceland a few days earlier.

Unprompted by me, he began sharing an animated description of the harrowing aspects of riding his motorcycle through the older tunnel on the way to the little village of Vidareidi. As he energetically elaborated on the oil spots on the raised middle portion of the lane, the sloped sides leading down to no shoulder, the complete absence of any light in the long dark passageway, and the presence of cars barreling down on him from behind, I found myself nodding, "Yes, yes, and yes!" Then when he said his bike slid out from underneath him and he wasn't sure if he was going to make it, I felt a huge sense of relief come over me. It was somehow comforting to know that this athletic, seasoned biker had encountered the same situation I had and felt similarly challenged.

Shortly afterward, Tim and Denise, two genial bikers from England I had also met in Seydisfjordur, joined our conversation and began describing the trials of riding through the wind in Iceland. Tim demonstrated how he had positioned his large muscular body on his bike, raising one hand toward the sky and lowering the other toward the ground, mimicking slanting his bike precariously in a desperate attempt to stay upright in the fierce Iceland gusts. He and his wife recounted that they weren't sure they would survive the ride. I looked at this experienced biker and his huge bike all loaded down with enormous bags, then at my much smaller bike, and realized it made all the sense in the world that I had asked myself the same question.

Heartened by their tales of adventure on Iceland and the Faroes, I was encouraged to learn that I was not the only rider intimidated by the deadly winds and hazardous tunnels.

My conversations with the other bikers that day validated the concerns I had with the condition of the older tunnel in the Faroes and the presence of the strong winds in Iceland, as well as the decisions I had made to mitigate my risks with those types of issues. It had indeed been the right call to "ride my own ride."

One of the best wrong turns ever! I didn't set out from Vinistra, Norway, intending to ride the Geiranger-Hellesylt ferry past this Seven Sisters Waterfall, flowing off the craggy cliffs into the glacier-fed lake below, but I'm so glad I did.

CHAPTER 15

LIFE IS SHORT, TAKE THE LONG WAY HOME

After disembarking from the ferry in Hirtshals, Denmark, I rode twenty-five miles to the Rabjerg Mile, a migrating, four million cubic meter coastal dune that moves up to eighteen meters a year. While there I stopped to walk through the undulating, forty-meter-high hills and to visit a fourteenth century church forced to close by the migrating sand. From there I traveled thirteen more miles east to Grenen, Denmark's most northeastern town, walking about a mile on the sand along the shoreline there to a small spit where the North Sea and Baltic Sea meet but, because of their different densities, do not merge. After a fantastic fresh-fried fish and vegetable lunch in nearby Skagen, I returned to Hirtshals to ride the ferry to Kristians and Norway and begin my push north to Nordkapp, the northernmost point of Europe accessible by road.

My first night in Norway was spent at the home of Erling and Ingunn Rafoss, members of a network called Bunk-a-

Biker that connects traveling motorcyclists with locals who offer up free lodging and sometimes food to visitors on bikes. I had stayed with quite a few Bunk-a-Bikers the previous summer in my travels through North America but had not found many hosts on this adventure who were at home, as so many Europeans travel extensively during July and August. I was especially grateful for Erling and Ingunn's hospitality, my first such stay of that journey.

Ingunn had graciously saved some homemade chili from dinner for me to eat after I arrived at their home from the ferry terminal in Kristiansand. While I ate, they both shared tips about potential routes north, as well as strong warnings about the perils of speeding in a country known for stiff fines and even jail sentences for those caught exceeding the posted limits.

After breakfast the following morning, I traveled north over 350 miles to Vinstra, riding through beautiful rolling farmland with multi-colored patchwork quilt crops, small villages with ships in the harbor, lakes and rivers framed by rolling hills, and what seemed like dozens of mountain tunnels.

The following morning, I headed northwest from Vinistra on what I anticipated would be a relatively short ride to the Trollstigen Road, a dizzy series of eleven mind-blowing hairpin curves and one of Europe's top riding destinations. As I worked my way north on Route E-6 from Vinstra and then west on Road 15, I found myself surrounded by a magical world of lush green meadows and trees, dark gray and blue river water the texture of velvet, rolling tufts of fog suspended in midair, and little villages nestled in valleys. At one point, a farmer tied a string across the road and proceeded to herd his dozen or so cattle from one meadow to another, taking one cow at a time as I waited.

Just when I thought I couldn't be more mesmerized, I turned north on Route 63 and found myself twisting and turning up and down a mountain pass on one of the best rides of my life. As I rose in elevation, the air became colder and crisper and the landscape changed from lush greenery to white-capped mountains, glacier-fed lakes and streams, and rocky outcroppings all around. Winding my way down the mountain toward the little village of Geiranger on an intricate series of hairpin turns, the foliage became greener and little houses dotted the hillsides on my left and right as the road furled out in front of me like a roll of ribbon tossed onto a table. As the trees cleared and the image of the sun-drenched town below became visible, my breath caught in my throat.

The view took my breath away when I rounded a tight turn descending the mountains above Geiranger and saw this collection of little buildings on the banks of the emerald-green colored fjord, huddled below the enormous mountains that rose out of the surrounding waters.

Nestled at the base of the mountain and set next to the fjord, the village was dwarfed by the enormous mountains surrounding it on all sides like a beautiful emerald showcasing all its hues of green—dark forest green-covered cliffs, light yellow-green meadows, and the silky blue-green of the fjord itself.

Blindly following my navigation app, I boarded the Geiranger-Hellesylt ferry, inadvertently heading in the opposite direction of where I hoped to go to reach Trollstigen. It had already taken me several hours longer than I expected to get to Geiranger due to the winding mountain roads and unexpected ferry delays, so I was becoming a little concerned that I might be finishing my day on a technically challenging road in fading light. However, determined to savor every moment of this "wrong turn," I focused on taking in more of the breathtaking scenery around me, enjoying the sunshine and spectacular water views.

The ferry turned out to be a mini cruise ship, with a cafeteria below and regular broadcasts from the helm informing us of one famous sight after another. My favorite was the Seven Sisters Waterfall, cascading in multiple streams off the rocky cliffs into the glacier-fed lake below and located opposite its "suitor" waterfall, the Friaren.

Disembarking, I traveled north and east to the visitor's center for Trollstigen as the sun went down in the sky and a thick blanket of fog began to appear around me. After stopping at the information center, I walked to several observation decks, hoping to get a clear picture of the famous narrow road snaking its way down the mountain but settling for a partial shot of the largely obscured path.

Back on the bike, I headed down the steep hillside, grateful that the time of day and poor visibility had resulted in less traffic behind me as I carefully wound my way around each of the tight switchbacks. Although I could see the road immediately in front of me, the views on either side were blocked by the dense fog. All that was visible to me in this stunning mountainous area was the pavement of the road in front of the bike and some of the low-lying bushes on the narrow shoulder. So I focused on safely navigating my way down to the base of the mountain, stopping briefly to rest at the bottom before heading to the neighboring village of Andalsnes, where my lodging for the night was located.

After dinner that evening, while enjoying a delicious dessert of almond merengue cake with lemon custard topping from Sodahlhuset, a charming little café near my hostel, I reflected on the irony that my day's journey to one of Europe's top riding attractions had turned out to be more spectacular than the famous road itself. I was grateful that I had taken the time to enjoy all the ride, rather than just focusing on my destination.

I also put some thought into where I wanted to travel the next few days. After safely circling Iceland and exploring some of that country's top natural wonders, my next key goal for the summer was to reach Nordkapp, the northernmost point of Norway. Aware that my flight out of Frankfurt was less than five weeks away, I was anxious to cross that landmark off my bucket list, wanting to ensure that I had time to travel through other European countries as well as hike in Switzerland before storing my bike at a motorcycle camp in Germany for the school year.

On the ferry from the Faroes I had met a sweet elderly couple in the ship's upper lounge who had strongly encouraged me to take a detour to visit the Lofoten Islands, a stunning archipelago in Norway near the Arctic Circle voted by *National Geographic* as one of the most appealing destinations in the world. After regaling me with tales of their travels all over the world, the wife had smiled at me with twinkling eyes shining through wrinkled, beautifully aged skin, patted me on the leg, and insisted I "simply must" visit Lofoten, telling me it was their favorite part of Norway.

Visiting this area would require substantially more time, money, and effort, as crossing to the archipelago by ferry was not easy to arrange and travel itself on the island would take a full day, putting me back on the road to Nordkapp two days later than I had anticipated.

I was conflicted about what to do, partially because I tend to be particularly goal driven and struggle to alter plans when I'm striving toward an objective, a tendency I've had since I was a young child. This singular focus has served me well in many senses—it made it possible for me to become my high school valedictorian, earn a presidential scholarship in college, gain admittance to one of the country's top five business schools, perform well in the corporate world, provide my children with an enriching and caring home environment, effectively teach my high school students, develop a thriving tutoring business, and become a published author.

However, in the few years I had spent motorcycling, I had begun to learn the value of being open to changes, having a sense of adventure and taking time to enjoy an unexpected detour when it presents itself. I even have a line of T-shirts that say "Life is Short, Take the Long Way Home," which I sell on my website. (*footnote*)

When bikers travel in groups, they often decide ahead of time what route to take and where to stop for lunch. Over delicious food, after catching up on each other's lives, the conversation invariably turns to what roads to take home. At that point in the day there are typically two kinds of options— riding directly back or taking a longer, more circuitous route on a particularly curvy back road or to an unusually scenic viewpoint.

When I first started riding and encountered this dilemma, I was often tempted to go straight home to have more time to finish household chores, complete projects, or tick more items off my to-do list. However, I learned over the years that I would invariably be happier at the end of the day if I spent more time on the bike. The chores would always be there, but the sense of well-being I felt from spending more time with the wind in my face was priceless. After taking the "long way" home, I found I had a deeper sense of peace and joy, was more patient with my loved ones, and had a greater optimistic outlook on life in general.

So, after reflecting on my options from my hotel room in Andalsnes, my path forward became clear. I made plans to

Available on the Shop tab at www.kathleenterner.com.

detour to the Lofoten Islands, arriving there in three nights after first traveling along the world-renowned Atlantic Ocean Road.

Leaving Andalsnes the next morning, I headed north on Route 64, breathing in the crisp, fresh country air and enjoying the beautiful rolling green mountains, dark gray-blue waters of the fjords, and little villages clustered on the edge of the water before boarding a short ferry from Herjestranda to Solsnes. From there I traveled by tunnel under the sea, took in more stunning, sparkling water views, rode a ferry to Molde, and followed the National Scenic Highway signs to the little town of Vevant, the starting point for the Atlantic Ocean Road, considered by many to be the "best road trip in the world."

Truly a case of a picture being worth a thousand words. The Storseisundet Bridge on the Atlantic Ocean Road appears to rise right into the sky before precipitously dropping back to earth.

Full of joy and anticipation for the treat that lay ahead of me, I headed out on what felt like a roller coaster ride on asphalt causeways, viaducts, and bridges connecting several islands to the mainland. After riding through much of the archipelago and enjoying the views of the rocky outcroppings and ocean waters, I stopped right before the Storseisundet Bridge to get pictures of this epic rise and fall of road. Looking at the overpass from either end, the pavement appears to lift into the sky and disappear. Passing over the bridge, I turned the bike around in Karvag to ride back from the opposite direction. As I neared the top of the precipitous rise, the wind howled in my ear, the sky darkened, my bike swayed under me, and I asked myself out loud, "What the heck am I doing here?"

Thrilled with the view and the experience, I settled into several good hours of riding through the countryside on my way to Trondheim, a picturesque little city with a historic bridge, quaint shops, and many restaurant choices.

The next day's ride to Bodo took me almost 450 miles north through dozens of tunnels, across a multitude of bridges, and along lakes, fjords, and rivers, passing landscapes in every possible shade of green—light green meadows, forest green trees, and dark green wildflowers topped in purple. The farther I traveled, the colder it got, and I began to see signs warning me of reindeer crossings.

After passing the towns of Mosjoen and Moirana, I pulled into the Arctic Circle Visitor Center, thoroughly enjoying my time in the warm, dome-shaped building, with its wide swath of pavers running down the middle of the floor at the exact latitude of the artic circle: 66°34'. The cheerful staff there provided me with envelopes postmarked from the Arctic Circle so I could mail letters and tufts of sheep's wool from the Faroe Islands home to my children and pit crew from the big, red post office box in the entryway. Friendly bikers outside asked to pose with me and the bike, intrigued that I had traveled all the way from Oregon to Norway.

I spent the night in Bodo and left the next morning, breathing in the fresh salty air of the Norwegian Sea, listening to the seagulls swooping above me, and looking forward to a day of meandering along the coast before catching my 4PM ferry to Moskenes on the southern tip of the Lofoten Islands.

As I traveled along Route 17, I passed through a variety of small islands with one sweet view after another of bays, rivers, waterfalls, and lagoons, all connected with a variety of tunnels and bridges. Little clusters of farmhouses sat on the banks of bays surrounded by green meadows and fields, wildflowers in vibrant colors of yellow and purple dotted the shoreline, and colorful combinations of white and gray storm clouds set against the mottled blue sky shifted with the breeze.

The small lagoons surrounded by barriers of rock and sand were particularly charming, their waters glittering in delightful colors of blue, green, aqua, and gray as they rippled back and forth with the wind. It was wonderful to have extra time to stop and enjoy these natural wonders, sit on the rocks, listen to the sound of the water lapping by my feet, and admire the striations in the boulders made over time.

I stopped in the tiny village of Kjopstad for a small lunch before turning around and heading back to Bodo for my ferry. After boarding the ship and working through a mishap with another biker who accidentally dropped his heavier bike on top of mine, I settled in for the ride to Moskenes, where I arrived late in the evening.

I checked into my hostel on the island and was fortunate enough to get a table at Restaurant Gammelbua, the only dining establishment still open in Reine. What a treat! The fish dumpling with ricotta and vegetables was crispy on the outside, creamy on the inside, and delicious, with lemon-honey sauce. The stockfish entrée with truffle seaweed Sandefjord butter was slightly browned, moist, tender, and fell apart on my fork. I was already getting a taste for how delightful this side trip might be.

My ride north through Lofoten the following day was one of the most pleasant, enjoyable, and visually appealing of my life, with hundreds of million-dollar views, well-paved roads that twisted and turned and dipped and soared, and warm afternoon weather complemented by blue skies.

Just a block away from my youth hostel, this little fishing village, dwarfed by the Lofoten mountain peaks above, provided a striking start to one of the best riding days ever.

The route was chock full of one stunning view after another, beginning just blocks from the hostel when I stopped in the early morning fog to gaze at the enormous Lofoten mountain peaks rising straight out of the waters of the picturesque little harbor of the village while fishing boats bobbed in the placid waters.

The waves of the Atlantic Ocean swelled to my right as I headed north on Route 10 while dozens of little bays, coves, and lakes appeared on my left. The various bodies of water came in more colors of blue than I could imagine—light blue, light green-blue, dark green-blue, purple-blue, and gray-blue. The water shimmered and sparkled, much of it smooth like a wet mirror, glistening under the now cloud-dotted but sunny sky.

Beautiful dark rocky outcroppings stood in stunning contrast to the blue waters around me—sheer cliffs covered in trees rising out of the edges of the bays, mounds of rock-covered dirt creating little islands in the coves, and smaller collections of rocks lurking just below the surface in the almost clear water of various sheltered inlets.

The road itself was a visual delight—a slew of variety as the often orange or green colored pavement curved around bodies of water, dipped under the sea in more than one underground tunnel, and rose into the sky on multiple suspension bridges, one of which seemed taller than any I've ever ridden on.

Rather than stop anywhere for lunch and miss out on any of the amazing views, I pulled my bike over to the side of the road and smeared brie cheese on leftover bread from the previous night's dinner, while soaking in the sun and looking out at the water.

Rather than take time off this glorious road to eat in a restaurant, I ate a snack on my bike and gazed at the surroudning wildflowers.

I couldn't help thinking how grateful I was that I had taken the time to visit this island paradise on my way to Nordkapp. Much of the riding so far that summer had been grueling, with frigid temperatures, raging winds, drenching rain, and challenging riding surfaces. The beautiful and peaceful journey along this collection of islands off the western coast of Norway had provided a welcome respite, a feast for the eyes, and a balm to my soul.

There would always be another destination to push toward, another goal to tackle, another item to check off the bucket list. Reaching Nordkapp was an accomplishment I was looking forward to. But I was glad I'd had the sense of mind to take the long way there.

Reluctantly leaving the Lofoten Islands, I headed east to Narvik for dinner and lodging. My meal at Furu Gastropub was the perfect end to a magical day. The cold yogurt soup with poached egg, beetroot, cucumber, and onion was one of the best appetizers I've ever had—light and flavorful but still filling enough to take the edge off my hunger. My steak was tender and juicy, cooked a perfect medium-rare, and just what I needed to fuel up for the next day's ride.

Victory! After battling thick fog, driving rain, frigid temperatures, and failed navigation, I reached the northernmost point in Europe accessible by road, one of three top destinations of my summer journey.

CHAPTER 16

NORTH TO NORDKAPP

After a great night's sleep, I loaded up the bike to push 300 miles north to Olderfjord, just two hours south of Nordkapp. Winding my way past dozens of little fjords and up, over, and through many mountain passes, I marveled at the different shades of blue in the water, the striking contrast the glacial waterfalls made as they cascaded down from the top of the rocky cliffs, and the efficiency with which Norway's engineers created so many different tunnels and bridges.

As I got closer to Olderfjord, the air grew colder, the fog thicker, the rain heavier, and the signs warning of reindeer crossings more numerous. Having never seen one in real life, I was absolutely delighted to come across three different herds of them on the side of the road just an hour south of my destination. With cute, small, white faces, enormous antlers, and white- and gray-mottled fur, these striking animals somehow camouflaged themselves perfectly in the scrubbier trees at the higher elevation.

What a glorious sight! The varicolored gray and white fur on this herd of reindeer helped them to be almost completely camouflaged in the scraggly trees surrounding them.

Because I knew I would not make it to my lodging in time to eat at the only restaurant in town, I stopped at a gas station café fifteen miles south of the hotel, where I was thrilled to find a savory, hearty, homemade, piping hot, creamy soup chock full of generous portions of fresh salmon and cod and topped with sprigs of dill. The attendant there even made a new batch of bread for me to eat for breakfast the next morning along with some smoked salmon I had found at the gas station's mini grocery store. I had been surprised to learn on this trip how common it was in Europe for gas stations to have delicious, fresh food offerings, from a large salad bar at an Orkan service center in Iceland to the freshly grilled burgers with numerous toppings offered at one of my first fuel stops in Norway.

I had envisioned an easy ride to Nordkapp the next day, as it was just two hours from my hotel and the roads I'd be traveling were paved. What I hadn't understood was that the path I was taking ran along the edge of the Porsanger Fjord, an inlet of the Arctic Ocean, allowing strong ocean gusts to sweep across the pavement and up the plateau on the other side, howling in my ear and threatening to topple my bike. With fog as thick and heavy as a wet wool blanket, frigid temperatures, and incessant rain, it felt as if I was riding in Iceland all over again. Grateful for my electric jacket and gloves and the experience I had gained earlier in the trip, I kept the bike in fourth gear, maintained a constant speed of forty-four miles per hour to stay upright but not lose friction with the road, flipped my face shield all the way up, pulled my goggles away from my face, and swiped the fog off my lenses every few seconds. Because it was so wet and windy, I was able to tilt my head sideways and open my mouth to drink anytime I got thirsty.

Despite the severity of the weather, the ride had its bright moments. On a couple occasions the haze briefly lifted, and I could glimpse the striking light blue color of the sea water to my right with the fog looming over it. A four point three-mile undersea tunnel from the mainland to the island of Mageroya, where Nordkapp is located, provided a delightful respite from the wind and rain.

About fifteen miles before I reached my destination, my navigation shut off, something another biker had warned me might happen. Although I wasn't worried about which road to take, I was concerned about safely steering the bike around curves without any advance notice of changes in my path, since I could see only a few feet in front of me.

After quite some time, I made out a sign on the side of the road notifying me that the entrance to the Nordkapp Visitor Center was 500 meters away. Then suddenly, out of the thick mist, a ticket booth materialized, a surreal appearance amid nothingness, making me wonder if I was a participant in a horror movie film about a wrong turn gone bad.

Walking through the well-lit, warm building to the iconic globe monument behind it, I experienced a sense of jubilation that I had made it this far, to a spot many consider to be the edge of the earth. Although I hadn't anticipated such a challenging riding day, it somehow seemed appropriate to have to battle the elements to reach the place where Europe ends and the Arctic Ocean begins. As I posed in the cold rain in front of the famous sphere-shaped landmark overlooking the fogged-in seas, I raised my motorcycle helmet high in victory. Although it was July 19 and I had left home less than a month before, it felt like I had already experienced a lifetime of adventure.

Leaving Norway and Finland behind, I headed south to Sweden, where an encounter with a hotel employee caused me to reevaluate how I would spend the remainder of my time on this summer's journey.

CHAPTER 17

SHIFTING GEARS IN EUROPE

After shopping for souvenirs and enjoying a warm meal with piping-hot tea at the visitors' center, I headed a few hours southwest to Alta to spend my last night in Norway before heading south to Finland, Sweden, and beyond. Grateful to have successfully circled Iceland and to have reached the northernmost point of Europe, I took some time that evening to shift gears and work out some of the details of the next leg of my summer journey. I booked a ferry from Stockholm to Estonia a few days later, and scheduled a service appointment for Adventure Baby in Tallinn, the capitol of Estonia.

I wasn't sure yet what countries I might visit before leaving my bike in Frankfurt, Germany, and flying home on August 20. I had a general plan to head south from Estonia through Latvia, Lithuania, and Poland and then west toward Switzerland, where I was looking forward to staying for a few days to enjoy some of my favorite hikes and familiar food. But

I was excited about keeping my itinerary largely open and waiting to let the adventures unfold naturally as I progressed down the road.

I realized I had a little extra time when I left Alta, so I decided to make it a short day on the road, allowing me to spend the night in Enontekio, Finland, and taste some of the local food. The ride there past thick forests of evergreen trees and a variety of rivers and lakes was cold and wet, but almost half of the motorists I passed heading the other direction were bikers who always took the time to wave in greeting.

Arriving in Enontekio, I stopped for snacks at the town's grocery store before checking in with the friendly non-English-speaking workers at my hotel across the street. Although I could use a translation website on my iPhone to communicate essential information, the staff's kind gestures made it unnecessary most of the time. When I held up my ripped and water-logged map, they cheerfully brought me tape and helped me put the pieces back together. Grateful for my dinner business at their on-site restaurant, they delivered plates of generously portioned food to my table with a flourish.

After dinner, I booked my room at the Pitea Golf Hotel in Sweden for the following night, completely unaware that the meaningful interactions I would have with the clerk there would change my perspective of the rest of my journey and result in one of the highlights of my trip.

My ride to Pitea started out in frigid temperatures and pelting rain and stayed that way. I traveled through one wooded area after another and alongside rivers and lakes, light green-colored meadows, and little farms. I took time to think thoughts of gratitude for my rainproof jacket, pants, and side saddlebags. Unfortunately, my waterproof riding boots proved to be no match for the relentless downpour, and I arrived in Pitea with the lower part of my jeans dripping wet and my socks soaked all the way through. Because I had no alternate pants or other knee-high wool socks, I hoped to find my hotel, quickly unpack my wet gear, and start drying out my clothes.

I had learned though my adventures so far that summer that checking into accommodations in Europe was often quite different than in the United States. Having traveled extensively through the forty-eight contiguous states and Alaska by bike, I had fine-tuned the check-in process in America, arriving at my well-marked destination for the night and then either parking in front of my motel room to quickly unload my luggage or pulling into the hotel parking lot and grabbing a cart to easily wheel my bags to my room. I found that it typically took less than fifteen minutes to get settled into my heated or air-conditioned lodging for the night.

I was surprised to find that this process in Europe often took me a full one to two hours, because the establishment had little or no signage alerting travelers to its presence, there was no parking available nearby for guests, I had to climb with my bags up to five sets of sometimes narrow steps to my room, or the unit itself was missing some essential amenity, such as a heat source, requiring me to make additional arrangements with the clerk of the facility.

When I arrived cold and soaking wet in Pitea, I gassed up the bike and purchased breakfast items for the following day before putting the hotel's address into my navigation. Arriving at that location, I could see golf course greens but no signs for lodging. After surveying the area, I was able to locate a red building with white doors that looked like the picture of the hotel I had seen in my booking app the night before. I decided to follow the small path from the main road to that spot.

Parking the bike and still seeing no signs for the hotel, I managed to locate a visitor to the golf course who said they thought I needed to go behind the structure where I was parked and across several lawns to find a clerk. So I rounded the building, my boots making a squishing wet noise with every step as I walked across a nicely manicured lawn, passed another building, strolled across another grassy area, and then traversed one of the holes of the golf course to arrive at a small shack set on the other side, still seeing no indicators of any kind for lodging.

Walking into the small hut, I saw a large, genial young man about my son's age with closely cropped hair wearing a Pitea Golf Course polo shirt and khaki pants. He was perched on a stool behind a counter with a row of keys over his shoulder and golf clubs set in stands off to the side. When I asked him if he knew where I could check in for the hotel, he gave me a welcoming smile, told me I was in the right place, and added, "No one can ever find me. We really should put up some signs."

Smiling inwardly at his comment, I explained my predicament with the wet clothes and asked if my room had a heat source so that I could warm up and dry my apparel. Even though the temperature had been in the forties and raining all day, Oscar informed me that the radiators in the room were turned off because it was summer, a refrain I had heard multiple times already on this year's adventure, often in frigid climates. After he offered to help me try to turn on the room's heaters, Oscar and I walked back across all the lawns with my toes becoming more waterlogged by the minute, only to confirm it was not possible to create any warmth in my room.

I asked if perhaps I could have a hair dryer, hoping to use the appliance to dry out the insides of my dripping wet boots and take some of the moisture out of my socks and jeans. Oscar said that the rooms did not have any hair dryers, but he offered to drive to his house and try to find one for me.

While waiting for Oscar to return, I set about to at least lay out my soggy items and organize some of my gear. After forty-five minutes had passed and Oscar still had not returned, I decided to get some dinner while I waited. However, when I closed the door to my hotel room, I realized Oscar had not left me the room key and I could not lock the door to protect my valuables. I walked past all the buildings and lawns I had passed earlier and saw Oscar strolling away from the hut on the other side of the golf course. Putting my hands up to my mouth to help my voice carry, I called out to him, asking if he knew where my room key was. He turned to me, grinned, looked at his hand, and held it up, exclaiming, "I've got it right here."

After getting my key from Oscar and walking past the buildings and lawns back to my room to lock up, I went to get dinner at the golf course's restaurant while waiting for the blow dryer, realizing that I would not have time to eat anywhere else that night. After a good, hot meal, I returned to my room to find all my clothes and the insides of my boots as wet as I had left them.

A few minutes later, while packing toilet paper in my boots to soak up some of the excess liquid, I heard a knock on the door and opened it to find Oscar standing there with a huge smile, triumphantly holding up the blow dryer he had found at his house and personally brought back to the room for me. I thanked him profusely, closed the door, and sat down on my bed to take stock of my situation.

At that point, it had been several hours since I had arrived. My feet were still waterlogged and my boots, socks, and pants dripping wet. I was cold and was not sure how to get warm, and it was tempting to focus on how wet and uncomfortable I was. But in reflecting on my interactions with Oscar, I realized that he had gone above and beyond his duties as an employee of the golf course to personally procure the blow dryer that I could use to start to dry out some of my items.

I realized I had an important choice to make. Did I want to focus on all the amenities that I did not have or to think about what I had to be grateful for? I was fortunate to have a dry roof over my head, a mattress to sleep on, hot running water, and electricity to charge my navigation and safety equipment. I had a full belly and provisions for breakfast. If I took a hot shower and put all the duvets from the room's two bunk beds on top of my mattress, I could crawl underneath them and get warm. The blow dryer would take some of the moisture out of my pants and socks, and the wool of the socks would help to keep my feet warm the next day even if they were still wet.

How did I want to remember my time here? Was I going to compare the check-in process with what I would normally encounter back home, looking for ways in which my current accommodation fell short? Or would I be able to focus on the positive, realizing that Oscar had gone out of his way to assist me? It was clear that he had a giving heart and a commitment to doing whatever he could to help me feel welcome and comfortable. His kindness in driving back and forth to his house and his generosity in loaning me his own blow dryer were remarkable and certainly not something I would expect of any employee, whether in Europe or America.

Thinking through what I had been learning so far on my summer journey, I realized that I could not substantially change the fact that it typically took one to two hours longer for me to get situated into a room in Europe than it did in the United States. Instead of expecting the countries I was traveling through to be more like home and getting frustrated when they weren't, perhaps it would be more constructive and appropriate to adapt my travel plans to the places I was visiting. I realized I could significantly shorten the riding time for each day, freeing up more time for me to be patient during the check-in process at my destinations and hopefully opening the door to having more unrushed conversations with the locals I met in the area. Although it would sometimes be a struggle for me to remain patient and calm in trying circumstances, I hoped the changes to my schedule would help me to improve my perspective.

Deciding to spend fewer hours on my motorcycle each day to make it easier to interact more positively with others felt very much like the decision I had made earlier in the year to adjust my travel plans out of respect for my daughter's wishes. Although I was disappointed about the impact it would have on my riding time, I also felt a sense of peace about my decision, knowing it was the right thing to do.

As a Christian, one of the two most important commandments given to me is to love others as I love myself. (*footnote*) It seemed like I had spent the last several years learning to see myself anew from God's perspective. Now that I was able to identify more as a person of value and strength, a person who could respond to fearful situations from a position of power rather than powerlessness, one who could find joy in the moment rather than fixate on shameful feelings about the past or worry about the future, I was more ready to turn additional focus outward.

The timing of this decision seemed appropriate, as the recent discovery of my brain tumors had already prompted me to reconsider my priorities. The four growths in my head provided a daily reminder to me that none of us really know how long we have left on earth. In thinking through how I wanted to spend the rest of my days, I knew that, as Jesus had said, in addition to loving God, there was nothing more important that I could do with my remaining life than to try to treat others with kindness.

Matthew 22:35–40, The Holy Bible: One of them, an expert in the law, tested him with this question: "Teacher, which is the greatest commandment in the Law?" Jesus replied: " 'Love the Lord your God with all your heart and with all your soul and with all your mind.' This is the first and greatest commandment. And the second is like it: 'Love your neighbor as yourself.' " (NIV)

*What better place to learn to slow down than ambling along
the cobblestone streets in Old Town Tallinn filled with colorful
buildings topped with turrets, church towers, and dormered roofs?*

CHAPTER 18

PROGRESS

I left Pitea on July 22, excited about what new adventures might lie before me as I traveled through several more European countries on my way to Frankfurt to catch my flight home a little less than a month later.

The rain that day was impressive, coming down so hard that it reminded me of a flash flood I had experienced in the Mojave Desert the year before. It was bouncing off the pavement like bacon grease on a hot skillet, obscuring my views of the odometer and navigation, and eventually causing my map app to quit completely. I found a car with bright headlights and followed it south toward Stockholm, stopping in the middle of a bridge on the way there to take a picture when blue sky finally peeked out from behind the storm clouds. An hour north of the capital, a huge rainbow appeared above me, a sign I saw as a promise of good to come.

So grateful to see blue skies after days of incessant rain and cold, I raised my hands upward in celebration while stopped on this suspension bridge in Sweden.

I spent two nights in the "Venice of the North," allowing me to visit the heart of the city, a collection of fourteen islands connected by fifty-seven bridges and sporting many charming canals and waterways. I wandered along the shoreline, ate a traditional Swedish meal at a little café as I watched the boats float by, learned about the fateful voyage of the Vasa museum's seventeenth-century ship, meandered along the cobblestone streets of Old Town, prayed in a medieval church, and watched the changing of the guard at the Royal Palace.

After a delightful overnight ferry ride from Stockholm to Tallinn, Estonia, I took Adventure Baby to a local Honda dealer for its scheduled maintenance and settled into a beautifully appointed and reasonably priced hotel room in the city, excited about spending several days traveling through Estonia, as all three of my children are fifty-percent Estonian on their father's side of the family.

Exploring Gamla Stan, the Old Town of Stockholm, I prayed in a medieval church, window-shopped at local businesses, and enjoyed a hearty portion of lasagna at an authentic Italian eatery while watching people walk past me on the uneven cobblestone streets.

On my way to dinner that night, I strolled the cobblestone streets of Old Town, admiring an eclectic combination of turrets, archways, steps, and colored buildings as I passed by the largest medieval artillery tower in the Baltic States and walked through Freedom Square before arriving at the Pegasus Restaurant.

My meal there was a gastronomic and visual feast, with each course incorporating an ideal blend of different, yet compatible, flavors, artistically presented. The bread was chock full of seeds, crispy on the outside, and served with creamy butter containing sizeable chunks of salt. My cold watermelon-tomato soup tasted sweet and spicy and was presented with watermelon seeds in its red center and a green coriander cream around the edges. The pan-fried halibut was topped with a crispy skin, included a flaky, moist center, and was accompanied by a spinach and snap pea mixture on top of a chorizo-butter sauce. The dessert of strawberry mousse contained flecks of blueberry meringue and was surrounded by a bed of mint milk.

As I savored each bite of my dinner, I also made it a point to engage in friendly conversation with my waitress, a tall young girl with long blonde hair, blue eyes, and rosy cheeks that reminded me very much of my daughter. She shared about her home life and some of the perspectives her fellow citizens had toward those in neighboring countries.

I had already begun to observe that I was making progress with the changes in my daily routine since Pitea—spending additional time at the gas pump answering questions from locals curious about my travels, engaging in extended conversations with reservation clerks, getting more input from residents about sightseeing opportunities, and lingering longer over my meals when opportunities for dialogue presented themselves.

From the capital, I traveled east the next day along the shoreline of Estonia, visiting a variety of small coastal towns and appreciating the fascinating juxtaposition of old and new that I could see both in the countryside and within city limits. Aged wood huts half buried in hills, ancient stone churches, a tall wooden windmill, and abandoned bunkers appeared side by side with glass and brick business buildings, metal wind turbines, and new cars bustling here and there. Within the same block in the small coastal town of Narva-Joesuu, I found a modern-day supermarket and a small wood shack with two local ladies selling fruits and vegetables for cash only. Arriving in the northeastern town of Narva on the border with Russia for the night, I posed with Adventure Baby for a photo of us at the checkpoint.

After receiving a hot tip from two bikers staying at my hotel, I decided the next day to travel briefly through Russia. I had not planned on visiting the country due to travel warnings issued by the US State Department. But Sven and Harold, two burly, affable motorcyclists from Sweden, had informed me of a small section of road from Estonia that was not patrolled by border agents and ran through the Russian Federation for a short period of time before returning to Estonia.

Giddy with excitement about the prospect of visiting what I had thought was an off-limits destination, I headed south past the small town of Lutepaa where I encountered a large yellow sign warning motorists, "You are entering the territory of the Russian Federation! Stopping vehicles and passage on foot prohibited within 1km." Apparently, it was okay to drive through the territory but not to stop in it! Having already gassed up and checked that all my gear was securely attached to the bike, I ventured off, passing through the short stretch of Russian land and continuing for several miles before turning around in Estonia.

Wow! Who would have thought that the woman who was too afraid to travel alone would be riding her bike by herself in Russia just three-and-a-half years later?

Returning the way I had come, I traveled back through Russia one more time before parking the bike to take a picture in Estonian territory just past the warning sign. Jubilant about safely making it in and out of Russia, I stood tall on the pegs of my motorcycle, gloves in hand, and arms held high in victory with a big grin on my face. Who knew that the girl who couldn't make it out of her driveway on her bike would be traveling to the Russian Federation by motorcycle just three years later?

While looking through the many delicious food offerings in Riga at Europe's largest bazaar, I had no idea that shortly afterward I would find myself lost on the outskirts of a military base!

CHAPTER 19

WRONG TURN THAT TRUMPS THEM ALL

I continued my circular loop around Estonia, noticing more countryside rich in history with decaying wooden windmills, crumbling stone churches, and old, splintered barns settling into the earth and surrounded by fields of hay and wildflowers in shades of purple, yellow, and white. As I traveled west to Pärnu, I rode alongside numerous paved bicycle paths filled with youth on scooters and bikes, pedestrians of all ages, and even those in wheelchairs. It was inspiring to see so many people of all different generations and walks of life spending time outdoors together.

From Pärnu I traveled north and west, crossing by ferry and bridge to the island of Saaremaa, where I lingered near the beach, climbed 242 steps to the top of the Sorve lighthouse to gaze out across the Irbe Straight toward Latvia, and stopped to enjoy a hot cup of tea with steamed milk at an outdoor table under the blue sky with the sun on my back. I was learning to slow down a little and more thoroughly enjoy the places I was visiting.

Resting after climbing 242 steps to the top of the Sorve lighthouse, I ordered a cup of hot tea with steamed milk to enjoy while gazing out at the Irbe Strait toward Latvia.

After spending the night in Kuressaare, I headed back across to the mainland and then south to Latvia along the coastline, appreciating the gorgeous views of the Gulf of Riga to my right and relaxing at a soft, white sandy beach surrounded by beautiful dunes and evergreen trees before heading into the city of Riga to explore the Central Market.

Navigating over uneven cobblestone streets, I parked the bike near the huge bazaar—Europe's largest—located in five pavilions constructed out of German Zeppelin hangars and situated on the Daugava River. Each hangar had a different category of food, from fruits and vegetables to raw meat, ready-to-eat delights, and other delectable items. Having ogled all the wares, I purchased what must have been a five-pound bag of fresh blueberries for six dollars before heading just north of Riga for dinner and lodging.

After eating a perfect medium-rare, dry-aged ribeye served with a creamy peppercorn sauce and three different kinds of coarsely ground salt at Vistinas Karbonades Steiki in Adazi, I got back on the bike for what was supposed to be a seventeen-minute ride to my room in the same town. I had called ahead of time to see if there were any logistical issues I needed to be aware of, and the clerk had informed me that Google Maps would not give me correct directions but that Apple Maps might be more accurate.

Heading out from the restaurant using Apple Maps to navigate, I became concerned just a few minutes later when the road I was on deteriorated significantly and I realized I was the only vehicle on it. As I jostled down the pathway trying to find spots of decent pavement between the massive potholes, I could see barbed wire fences to my left, thick forest to my right, and multiple warning signs including the word *Militars*, which sounded an awful lot like the word *military* to me. At that point I was hopelessly lost and wasn't sure which way to go. However, when the map app directed me to turn left down a muddy path in the middle of the forest, I knew I needed to park the bike and re-evaluate what to do.

As I stood next to my motorcycle in the dwindling light on the pockmarked roadway and prayed for guidance, I spotted an old white pickup truck bumping up and down the path toward me from the forest. Not sure who was inside but desperately hoping for help, I waved down the driver, a muscular man with closely cropped hair.

When I explained that I was lost and needed assistance, the gentleman tried to reassure me by telling me that I was on a military base and there were cameras everywhere watching me. It turns out I had stumbled on NATO's forward element in Latvia—a multinational, battalion-sized battlegroup base. The road was in disrepair because of all the tanks and heavy machinery operating in the area. Not especially comforted by his words, I asked if he might be willing to help me find my hotel.

Fortunately, Arthur spoke both English and Latvian and was willing to communicate with the hotel staff when I called them on my phone to determine their location. He offered to lead me there, and I gratefully accepted. As we turned off on a side road that I had passed over an hour earlier after leaving the restaurant, I noticed there was no signage pointing guests to the hotel. The first thing the clerk said to me when I arrived was, "No one can ever find us here." I chuckled to myself, realizing this wasn't the first time I had heard the refrain but grateful I had adjusted my schedule to make extra time for just these kinds of issues. I must say, though, when I changed up my riding routine a few days before, it never occurred to me I would need the extra hours in my day to find my way off the outskirts of a NATO military base.

Having never traveled to Poland before, I was unsure of what to expect. I couldn't have been happier when my navigation ended up directing me on small country roads past dozens of little villages, with dogs running in the street, storks preening in their nests, and ancient buildings on both sides.

CHAPTER 20

COUNTRY ROADS AND FARMHOUSE FEAST

Grateful to have safely reached my lodging the night before, I headed south in the morning to travel through Latvia and Lithuania and into Poland. Riding past beautiful, amber waves of grain, lush green fields, crops of corn, and evergreen trees, I stopped to enjoy a traditional Lithuanian meal of meat pockets and roasted bacon with horseradish in Panevezys with a biker I had met at a nearby gas station before arriving in Suwalki for the evening.

I had hoped to spend a few days in Poland, but my support team back home was concerned about the rising tensions between Russia and neighboring Belarus and had urged me to make my way south to the Slovak Republic as quickly as possible. Kathy Nesper, Grant Myers, and Allen Nay had been providing me with round-the-clock assistance so far that summer, with Grant troubleshooting mechanical issues, Kathy helping with technical problems, and Allen providing prayer support. Grant and Kathy had both been part of my safety crew for the previous three summers, and Allen, a kind biker and retired Marine with a gentle voice and long white beard was a new member to the pit crew. Because he lived in a different time zone and had a different sleep schedule than the other two, I was always able to reach one of the three.

Heeding their advice, I planned to ride over 400 miles to the Slovak Republic after stopping for a pizza lunch in Radzymin with fellow motorcycle adventurers Travis and Chantil Gill, who had reached out to me a few days earlier via Facebook Messenger asking to meet. I had first connected with Travis and Chantil the previous January, when I called them to get their input about arranging to have a bike titled in my name in Europe. They had kindly shared some of their strategies and offered to stay in touch. Chantil had subsequently given me advice about riding boots, and Travis had shared numerous stunning photos of the beautiful places they both had visited on their motorcycles.

After making good time for several hours on the motorway, I pulled over next to their heavily-laden BMW G650GSs at Restauracja La Pasta Pizza and Pasta just north of Warsaw, where Chantil rushed out to greet me, her shoulder-length, light brown hair framing her friendly face, twinkling eyes, and big grin. Travis, brawny and tanned from riding in the sun, stood up to shake my hand, his smile framed by a salt and pepper beard and mustache.

It was wonderful to be able to speak English with fellow Americans, enjoy a delicious, wood-fired pepperoni pizza, and share stories of our biking adventures. When Chantil offered to pray over our food, it opened the door for some thought-provoking conversations about our goals and what messages we hoped to convey to the followers of our blogs.

After traveling a few more hours by motorway after lunch, my navigation prompted me to accept an alternate route and proceeded to lead me on a series of wonderful little backroads through over a hundred villages in southern Poland.

After spending several hours on motorways with speeding traffic, the patchwork quilt-colored farmlands on rolling hills on my way to Krynica Zdroj provided a welcome respite from the hustle and bustle.

What an unexpected treat! Rather than bombing down the freeway, I found myself navigating down small, one-lane roads with no center line, circling around dozens of roundabouts through little town squares, and riding up and down a variety of bridges over a series of rivers and lakes. Instead of trying to dodge cars traveling at speeds well over 150-percent of the posted speed limit, I found myself pulling over to get pictures of storks preening in their nest, braking to avoid dogs running out into the street, slowing down to smell the food being cooked nearby, parking to look at stone and brick churches, and stopping to admire clusters of country homes nestled in the foothills.

The next morning, after breakfast in Krynica Zdroj, I navigated west through the tiny hamlet's narrow streets to country roads covered by a canopy of trees and along the Poprad River, past little picturesque towns with colorfully painted buildings nestled on the banks. From there I continued to the city of Žilina, Slovakia, where I stopped for the night to rest and dry out gear still dripping wet from the relentless rain earlier in the day.

The manager of my hotel in Žilina, Slovakia loaned me this ladder to hang my soaking wet gear on and also provided me with extra toilet paper to stuff in my boots and helmet in an attempt to soak up the excess water.

After waking up and removing the toilet paper I had stuffed inside my formerly water-logged boots, helmet, and goggles, I continued west through the Czech Republic and into Austria, enjoying one delightful view after another of rolling hills, multicolored crops, beautiful lakes with small islands lit up in the late afternoon sun, clusters of little villages and the most beautiful sunflower field I have ever seen. Thousands of lush, green stalks and large, beaming yellow heads filled to the brim with seeds danced back and forth in the early evening breeze just before the Austrian border as I stood by the roadside mesmerized by the colors and movement.

My dinner that evening in the small hamlet of Kollerdorf was one I will never forget. My Austrian Bunk-a-Biker hosts escorted me down a cobblestone pathway to a local farmer's backyard restaurant, where we passed twinkling garden lights and marble-topped wine barrels before settling down at a picnic table. There we enjoyed a feast of several different freshly baked breads accompanied by a variety of flavorful cold meats and homemade, creamy and rich spreads made with eggs, potatoes, and cream cheese. Arno and Margit, who had welcomed me to their home earlier with open arms and even done my laundry, looked on in amusement as I kept polishing off one plate after another, making satisfied chewing sounds, and exclaiming, "This is just so good!"

This field of bright yellow sunflowers dancing atop thick stalks of green and blowing back and forth in the evening breeze just before the Austrian border was one of the most impressive floral displays I have ever seen.

Fortified with food and happy to be wearing clean clothes, I rode through the Austrian mountains to Zell am See the next day, swooping down and around one pass after another and admiring the lush green vegetation, rolling hills and towering granite peaks, beautiful rivers snaking along the foothills, and little villages situated in the valleys below the wispy fog. As I rode, I sang, "The Hills are Alive" and "Climb Every Mountain" at the top of my voice through the confines of my motorcycle helmet. These songs from *The Sound of Music* made so much more sense when traveling through the countryside where the movie was filmed.

Winding my way through the Austrian countryside, passing through little villages as I rode up and down one mountain after another, I couldn't resist singing "The Hills are Alive" at the top of my voice inside my motorcycle helmet.

When I awoke the next morning, I could see the foothills of the craggy Austrian Alps outside my window, circled by a wispy ring of fog and covered by dark clouds. After loading my bike, I rode west toward Liechtenstein, up and over one mountainside after another. The mist was quite beautiful. settling like a soft, white baby's blanket on little towns, hovering like whisps of cotton candy around the steeples of churches, and nestling in the clefts of the valleys like the lint in a clothes dryer. Cattle grazed peacefully in the alpine pastures, and wood chalets decorated with hanging pots of bright pink geraniums dotted the rolling hills and thickly forested slopes of the peaks around me.

As I passed the Arlberg ski area, the temperature dropped noticeably, and the trucks in front of me struggled to maintain their forward momentum up the steep grade. As I crested the top of the pass, I couldn't decide what excited me more: the glorious views of the rocky, snow-topped Alps on the horizon or the picture on my GPS of the road to Liechtenstein in front of me—one tight switchback after another, cascading down the mountain like a pile of spaghetti heaped on a plate. After descending the mountain and entering Lichtenstein's capital city of Vaduz, I enjoyed a hearty meal from a local restaurant before settling my head on the pillow to sleep, giddy with anticipation that I would be traveling to Nyon, Switzerland, the next day, a little city in Europe that I consider to be a second home.

My plan to spend several days in Nyon, Switzerland, a little town where I had created so many wonderful memories of my grandmother, turned out to be fortuitous due to unexpected mechanical difficulties with the bike.

CHAPTER 21

A GRANDMOTHER'S LOVE

After a restful night in the capital of Liechtenstein, I woke filled with excitement about leaving for my destination for the night, a small pedestrian-friendly town with cobblestone streets, medieval towers, and little shops about a half-hour east of Geneva. For years, I had visited my Swiss grandmother there, spending my evenings enjoying dinner and good conversation with her, my days hiking in the surrounding mountains, and sampling the treats at local restaurants. Grannie, an avid hiker and adventurer in her younger days, loved to hear the details of my exploits every evening, drinking in each word, asking for more details, and making restaurant recommendations for the places I might be hiking to.

My grandmother and I had always been close, as I had made it a point to visit her regularly starting from age five, when I flew from my home in California to New York with a family friend and then by myself from New York to London to see Grannie at her home there. Although Grannie was over fifty at that time, she interacted with me with the enthusiasm and care of a much younger person. She skipped down the cracked city sidewalks holding my hand, exploring gardens and parks with me while I delightedly licked orange cream popsicles. She pointed out the types of ducks floating by on the lake and birds settled on the tree branches overhead and arranged for me to ride horseback along the city's many park trails. She would sit on the oriental rug in her living room with me to play Chutes and Ladders.

On previous visits to Swizerland, Grannie and I had enjoyed numerous delicious meals together at a variety of local restaurants while I regaled her with tails of my hikes during the day and she shared stories of her youth.

I continued spending time with Grannie at her homes in London and Switzerland throughout my youth, shopping at Harrods in the city and skiing the Swiss Alps in winter or hiking them in summer, with Grannie always taking a keen interest in my growth and development. On one particularly memorable occasion as a teenager, my grandmother was attempting to teach me and my younger brother some of the finer points of proper table etiquette in a fancy restaurant. My brother, finding all the rules and restrictions rather humorous, started laughing so violently the milk he was drinking squirted out his nose and all over the white cloth-covered table festooned with fine china. As always, Grannie took the unexpected development in stride, lovingly but pointedly bringing order back to our gathering.

When I grew older, I began to appreciate how strong and adventurous my grandmother was. She shared how she fell into a crevice while hiking on ice in her seventies, described night skiing by moonlight as a youngster, and detailed how she had worked several jobs as a single parent raising my mother. She had left her abusive husband after he punched her in the face, breaking her nose. Looking at my grandmother's silky, porcelain skin, perfectly coifed ash-blond hair, meticulously sculpted fine eyebrows, neatly outlined red lips, and brightly twinkling blue eyes, it was hard to imagine all the obstacles she had overcome and adventures she had been on. Although quite petite and small boned, she had a sense of authority about her that caused even the brawniest men in her presence to acquiesce to her wishes.

As she aged, her eyes deteriorated and she was unable to read letters anymore, but I was able to stay in touch with Grannie between visits by calling her and recording messages onto CDs and mailing them to her. Even well into her mid-nineties, her mind was sharp as a tack, pointing out any inconsistencies in my story if I tried to be evasive about activities that might concern her.

Unfortunately, in 2017 when Grannie was ninety-eight years old, she had a bad fall, was diagnosed with dementia, and was placed in a nursing home in Switzerland. Because she had previously expressed to her caregivers that she would not want me to interact with her if her mental capacities were diminished, it was decided that it was in Grannie's best interest for me not to communicate with her anymore.

When I first found out I would no longer be able to speak with Grannie, I was heartbroken. I had called her frequently over the course of my lifetime, and she had always responded to my calls enthusiastically, calling me "darling," telling me that she was just thinking of me, and letting me know how happy she was to speak with me. Although the frequency of my calls to her had ebbed and flowed over the years, it was comforting to know that she was always there and that she loved me so wholeheartedly. It was fortunate that I had mailed her several CDs over the months before her dementia diagnosis, sharing uplifting details about my life, affirming my love for her, and thanking her for the positive impact she'd had on me.

Although I wanted to honor her wishes and those of her caregivers, I missed my grandmother deeply. I struggled to accept the fact that she was alive but I couldn't tell her I loved her. I grieved the loss of her voice and presence in my life, oftentimes dreaming that I had seen her, only to wake up crying when I realized we were still separated.

As I rode toward Switzerland on my motorcycle that day, my feelings were mixed, as I was excited about visiting the place where Grannie and I had so many positive memories but sad that she would not be experiencing the small town and surrounding areas with me. In a break from my typical travel pattern, I had booked five nights in the same place, allowing plenty of time to explore and reflect on all that my grandmother had contributed to my life. I would be taking a mini-vacation at a small hotel in the middle of the pedestrian area of Nyon, where Grannie and I used to sit listening to the birds sing, giving myself the opportunity to walk, shop, and eat in the places where she and I had spent so many hours together. While making my way toward my lodging there that day, I had no idea how fortuitous it was that I had not planned to do much riding over the next several days.

I traveled past the rippling gray-blue Rhine River, the silky-smooth waters of Lake Walensee, and the tiny village of Niederbipp, with little houses situated on large plots of lush green farmland surrounded by towering Swiss mountains. I continued past Lake Bierlersee, sporting tiny white sailboats bobbing on its surface and passenger ships ferrying tourists back and forth between the patchwork crops located on both banks and below more beautiful, white-tipped mountains.

Forty minutes later, while riding eighty miles an hour in heavy traffic in the middle lane near Corcelles-Pre-Concise, my bike abruptly lost power, completely shutting down my engine and making it impossible for me to maintain speed with the semi-trucks and cars surrounding me. I managed to steer the bike to the side of the road, coasting onto the shoulder without colliding with any vehicles. I was relieved to be safe, as I had traveled through dozens of tunnels earlier in the day, many of which only had one lane and no shoulder, making a mechanical breakdown there potentially disastrous.

Another motorcyclist pulled over to check on me, and we both thought that perhaps low oil was an issue, because my oil warning light had come on. After putting more oil in the reservoir, I continued toward Nyon, hopeful that the bike was in good working order.

Unfortunately, ten minutes later as I was heading south toward Lausanne, the bike lost power and the oil warning light came on again, requiring another evasive maneuver to make it to the safety of the shoulder. I was concerned about the warning indicator, since I knew the oil tank was full. Thankfully, Grant Myers from my support crew back home was able to get me the phone number for a local tow truck driver who agreed to come out and look at the bike, along with an English-speaking mechanic friend who could troubleshoot the issue and help translate our conversation.

Not sure why my bike had stalled suddenly in the middle of speeding traffic, I was relieved to have this local tow truck driver and mechanic check out Adventure Baby before I proceeded on to Nyon.

Both these genial fellows showed up shortly, enthusiastically looking over the bike in their generously cut white T-shirts, rosy cheeks glistening with sweat in the heat of the afternoon sun while they deftly inspected the bike with their grease-stained hands. They determined that there was too much oil in the bike, removed some of it, and recommended I take it to a mechanic in Glans, near Nyon, before riding it much further. Although they felt the bike was safe to ride the half-hour left to my lodging in Nyon, they weren't sure why the oil warning light was coming on and felt it needed a more detailed inspection.

Fortunately, I was able to make it to the Hostellerie du XVI Siecle before the shops closed for the night that Saturday. I stored my bike in their garage and rushed off to the local market to get enough provisions to hold me over until the grocery stores re-opened on Monday, when I would also be able to reach the motorcycle mechanic in Glans, just a few miles away. It had been terrifying to lose control of the bike twice in the same day, and I was relieved that I had plenty of time not only to enjoy Nyon but also to work with the local bike shop to get my motorcycle back in road-worthy shape before continuing west.

Although it was foggy and rainy the next morning, I simply couldn't resist heading off on my favorite hike of all time, traveling up to an elevation of 3,415 feet via a little red mountain train from Nyon to St. Cerque and then hiking another 1,600 feet up through the Swiss countryside to eat at my favorite restaurant in the world—a little chalet-styled establishment called La Barilette. The eatery serves a rich and flavorful cheese fondue and homemade fruit desserts and offers a breathtaking view of the French Alps from its outdoor dining patio. I figured that I would enjoy the physical exercise and food, even if I wasn't able to see the mountains through the rain and fog.

One of the things I love about hikes in Switzerland is that following the yellow trail markers is a little like going on an Easter egg hunt—you know what you're looking for, but you don't always easily find it. The brightly colored indicators are posted in a variety of shapes and locations, some easier to see than others. The signage can be as simple as a black arrow in a yellow diamond on a rock or as modern as a yellow street sign with the name of the destination and estimated time to arrival. Sometimes the markers are in front of you, but other times you must look up or behind you to find them.

I decided to think of this hike through the mist as a reconnaissance mission—an opportunity to try to find the trail I had traveled years ago before my intended attempt on Wednesday, a day that I anticipated would be much sunnier and allow for better views. I recalled some of the details— turn right in town just before the large pink building, go behind a local's back lawn, head uphill, pass through a lumber yard, go down a small residential road, hike through several cow pastures, and then climb up several rocky inclines.

After making one wrong turn down a deeply rutted muddy path and getting drenched by the incessant rain, I was delighted to eventually find the familiar old restaurant at the Dole Summit. I sat at my favorite table, catching up with the waiter, who remembered me from the past, and ordering the piping hot cheese fondue served with crusty thick bread slices still warm from the oven. As I broke off generous pieces of the flavorful fresh bread and swirled it in the creamy Vacherin-Gruyere mixture, my taste buds danced with joy. The dessert was a juicy and mildly sweet concoction of fresh apricots topped with a crispy crumble that perfectly balanced the heavier meal.

Even though the French Alps remained hidden in the white and gray mist, the clouds parted shortly after I finished my meal, making it possible for me to get a glimpse of Lake Geneva down below. I reflected how grateful I was to be enjoying such wonderful food after an invigorating hike and to be in a place that held such meaning for Grannie and me.

The following day, I contacted the mechanic in Glans to make an appointment for my bike for the next morning before traveling by ferry across Lake Geneva to Yvoire, France. This preserved fortified village is one of the country's most beautiful destinations, with bright pink and red geraniums bursting from thousands of planters placed strategically along the old cobblestone paths and on the ancient brick and stone buildings, earning it an international trophy for landscape and horticulture.

The boat ride across Lake Geneva was incredibly restful, gliding across the placid lake waters with the bright blue sky above me, the mild summer sun warming my back, the beautiful, white-tipped Swiss mountains behind me, and the French Alps rising in front. Arriving in Yvoire, I climbed up the hill to the center of town, admiring the sight of Yvoire Castle, built in 1036, and taking my fourth left onto Rue de l'Eglise to arrive at La Creperie D'Yvoire, a small eatery that serves freshly made savory and sweet crepes in every possible flavor.

This village in France is considered one of the country's most stunning, as it is filled with thousands of planters overflowing with colorful flowers draped on the walls of the crumbling stone buildings.

After a picturesque boat ride across Lake Geneva, I savored every bite of my lunch crepe with ham, three cheeses, spinach, and cream, as well as my dessert crepe filled with butter, sugar, and lemon at La Creperie D'Yvoire.

I waited a few minutes for one of the kid-sized tables on the outdoor front patio to become available, as Grannie had always insisted that these were the best seats in the house, with a direct line of sight for people-watching and gazing at the flower-covered stone buildings across the way. Sitting at the squat, rustic table with my knees bunched up under me, I ordered a lunch crepe with ham, three cheeses, spinach, and fresh cream, as well as a desert crepe served with butter, sugar, and lemon juice. I was glad not to be rushed through my meal, as I savored every bite of what Grannie and I always believed were the best crepes in the world.

The first order of business the next day was to take Adventure Baby to the mechanic in Glans to troubleshoot my mechanical issues. The time there was rather frustrating at first, as the mechanic drained some of the excess oil from my bike, did a cursory inspection, and pronounced the bike good to go.

I had learned from my interactions with service professionals in the past that it was important to make sure mechanical problems had been fully resolved to my satisfaction before I left the dealership, even if it meant that I had to be in the unenviable position of asking a technician to do work they didn't feel was necessary. I wasn't comfortable taking the bike back to Nyon with me until the mechanic in Glans had identified why my engine had shut off twice in the same day, and I explained to him that I would not be leaving until I felt the bike was safe to ride.

He agreed to investigate the problem a little further, checking the battery and doing an electronic diagnostic test but not finding anything suspicious. After a test ride with the bike, however, he returned with a big grin on his face, declaring he had identified the problem. Apparently, the after-market kickstand I installed on my bike when I had it lowered several months earlier in Oregon had become clogged with grit and was not fully retracting when it was flipped up. The bike had a "safety" feature that shut the engine off and turned the oil warning light on when the kickstand lowered slightly during a ride. It seems that the vibration from the bike while I traveled through Switzerland a few days earlier had caused the loose kickstand to lower a little and the motor to turn off.

The mechanic thoroughly cleaned and oiled the kickstand, making sure it could fully retract, before I left with the motorcycle, grateful to have identified what had caused the earlier power loss.

Later that day, while hiking along Lake Geneva from Morges to Lausanne, I spent some time thinking about what I had learned about the bike. As I strolled along the pedestrian walkway past small sailboats gaily bobbing in the lake, white swans with gray cygnets preening on the shore, planters chock full of brightly colored flowers, and families relaxing on the sandy beaches, I realized that the kickstand might still pose a safety risk even when oiled, as it was an after-market part not specifically manufactured for my machine and might continue to loosen when jostled enough.

The mechanic had mentioned in passing that morning that it was possible to disconnect the kickstand sensor. I thought it through and decided that I would rather accept the risk my kickstand might lower somewhat while I was riding without me knowing it than to continue traveling with a "safety feature" that would shut off my bike in that eventuality. So, while on the train back from Lausanne to Nyon late that afternoon, I called the mechanic and arranged to bring the bike in on Thursday before I left town so he could disengage the sensor.

Relieved to be feeling even more confident about my plans with the bike, I headed out to dinner that evening along with two dear family friends to eat at Auberge de Luins, a small local restaurant I had frequented with Grannie in the past, enjoying rich hearty servings of Malakoff. This cheese delight is typically only found in a few small villages in the country and is created with Gruyere cheese and egg that is deep fried in a hemispherical mound atop a piece of white bread. I savored every crunchy bite with dabs of mustard, relishing the feel of the creamy cheese oozing out into my mouth and knowing it might be quite some time before I had the opportunity to enjoy the delicacy again.

The next day was my last full day in Switzerland, and I elected to use it to hike up to La Barilette once more, this time in the warm summer sun with blue skies above. As I walked along the dirt pathway past the now-clear million-dollar views of Lake Geneva and the French Alps, dodged enormous cow dung patties in the pastures, climbed up steep rocky inclines, and listened to the melodic tinkling of cowbells from fields in all directions, I reflected on how bittersweet the day was. It had been so wonderful to explore many of the places that Grannie and I had been to, but it was also hard to know that I was located just minutes from her nursing home and still unable to see her.

I call the patio of La Barilette my "Happy Place," as I can think of few locations I would rather be than enjoying a steaming hot bowl of creamy cheese fondue while gazing at the white-tipped alps of France.

Although it was my desire to honor her wishes, I had hoped that something might change while I was in Switzerland, that perhaps her caregivers, knowing I was in the country, might reach out to me with an invitation to visit Grannie. I had an intense yearning to hold her and comfort her and had prayed fervently that God would open a door for me to spend time with her, but no opportunities had been made available. I left town thinking that there was no hope for me to ever see my beloved 105-year-old grandmother again. Little did I know that less than six weeks after my return to the United States, God would "open the door" for me to connect with her in a way that could only be described as miraculous.

Famous for its spectacular setting as well as its gravity-defying abbey, the island of Mont-Saint-Michel in France seemed to be a fitting stop near the end of my trip as I wound my way back to Germany to catch my flight home.

CHAPTER 22

GRAND FINALE

While at my hotel in Nyon, I had put some thought into how I wanted to spend my last ten days in Europe before my August 20 flight back to America from Frankfurt. I reached out to a variety of bikers worldwide for tips on spectacular riding destinations and had received numerous suggestions. However, the road that most intrigued me was the N2 in Portugal, a 739-kilometer scenic byway that ran all the way from Chaves in the far north to Faro on the Algarve coastline in the south. The opportunity to ride this breathtakingly beautiful route was made even more enticing when Gary Medin, the Facebook friend from Minnesota who had given me so many good tips for riding in Iceland, reached out via Messenger to let me know he was also headed to Portugal and could join me there. He and I had been communicating back and forth with messages and phone calls throughout the summer but had not yet met in person.

Since I knew I needed to be back in Germany with time to spare for my flight home, I decided to cover the over 1,000 miles from Nyon to Portugal in two days, traveling mainly on freeways and stopping only briefly in Ychoux, France for food and lodging before continuing through Spain. The trip southwest took me over a variety of beautiful bridges and viaducts, crossing over many rivers and streams, riding alongside lakes and fields of corn, wheat, and sunflowers, the latter leaning into the sun and gently blowing in the wind. As I rode further south, the heat intensified and the landscape became more barren and brittle.

Crossing over into Portugal, time seemed to slow down. Traffic merely meandered along narrow streets in the towns I passed through, customers at the gas station took their time talking to one another before getting back in their cars, and the clerk at the local grocery store stopped to ask what meal I would be preparing with my groceries.

Choosing where to travel for my last few days on the road this summer was not easy. But the allure of the N2 scenic byway, running south from Chaves Portugal through little villages and towns and alongside postcard-perfect mountains and rivers, was hard to beat, not to mention the opportunity to ride with Facebook Friend Gary Medin, who planned to be in the country at the same time.

I met up with Gary at a local restaurant that did not even begin preparing our food until forty-five minutes after we ordered, giving us plenty of time to catch up on our summer travels and make plans for the next day. I have always enjoyed my conversations with Gary because his positive perspective and enthusiasm for riding are contagious.

Our first stops the next morning were at the sticker-covered N2 kilometer marker 0 and at one of the larger, iconic yellow signs, where we took photos before heading toward Vila Real. From the very beginning, this route through the rural heartland of Portugal provided one visual treat after another. Heading through the first few small villages, I could see the road snaking back and forth among the houses and farms in front of me while trees formed a canopy of shade above.

My jaw dropped when I first turned my head to the right to take in this vast expanse of intricately lined vineyards snaking down the mountainside to the valleys below.

As we headed farther south, the valley to our right opened to provide a vast, sweeping view of dozens of beautifully terraced and manicured vineyards on the sides of the sloped foothills, with villages clustered at the base and the Marao mountain range rising above them all. The lush green vines, neatly plotted and trimmed in such intricate patterns on every cleft and hill, simply took my breath away. After two days of taking main roads in the searing heat, I was chortling with joy as Gary and I swooped down, up, and around one glorious mountain curve after another, passing more stunning valleys and vineyards, as well as rivers and farms on our way south. There seemed to be almost a celebratory mood among the other motorists we passed on the road—cars honked, motorcyclists waved, and everyone pulled over to capture images of the stunning views.

North of Lamego, Gary and I took a detour on Route 222 to follow the Douro River as it snaked along to the west before turning around and continuing south. After we passed the 100-kilometer marker on N2, the landscape became less mountainous and green and was replaced by amber rolling hills, beautiful in their own right.

Returning to Lamego, Gary and I settled into a youth hostel before walking to dinner at Casa Philippe, where we thoroughly enjoyed one of the best meals of the summer for both of us, a generous portion of tender and moist "little goat" served with savory potatoes cooked in butter, olive oil, peppermint, and the juices of the meat. We relished every bite as we shared stories of motorcycle adventure and hopes for our future travels. Our conversation flowed easily as we laughed about biking mishaps and recounted glorious roads we had inadvertently discovered in our journeys.

As I headed out of Lamego the next morning, with Gary continuing south toward Africa and me forging north toward my flight home, I found myself not wanting to leave the city's old stone buildings lining little narrow cobblestone streets, quaint shops and eateries, lively ambiance, and delicious food.

Heading toward Spain, I was transfixed by the stunning vistas of vineyards to the east—neat lines and swirls of light and dark green winding down the terraced slopes amid the trees and rocks, patches of other crops clustered in between, and little houses interspersed throughout. I paused several times to gawk and take pictures before finally resolving to move down the road.

After traveling on main roads for two hours, I turned off near Leon, Spain, entering an entirely different, stark world. The landscape became flatter and browner and filled with scrub brush. Traffic disappeared, and the roads narrowed and deteriorated. As I passed through several towns with no services or signs of life, I counted my blessings that I had happened to fill up right before leaving the main road and settled in to relish the solitude and the emptiness, looking for different shades of dirt and textures of vegetation. My phone stopped charging in the intense heat, and I sent up a prayer that my navigation would last until I reached my destination.

Approaching the Riano Regional Park, the road became more twisty, the land hillier, and a stunning vivid green-blue lake appeared beyond the dam to my left. Surrounded by large gray limestone mountains, the brightly colored body of water stood in stark contrast to the rocky formations above it.

After another fifty miles, the road rose in elevation, climbing up and then over a large mountain pass for another fifty or so miles to the city of Potas below. I stopped to take in the view from the top of the pass, relishing the sight of scrubby fields with wildflowers in the foreground and the majestic mountains rising through the clouds above me. I could hear cowbells tinkling in the distance as a local farmer rounded up his herd for the night. Descending on one switchback curve after another, I felt such enormous gratitude for yet another incredible day on the road.

When I threw open the wooden shutters on the window of my room in the small hamlet of Aliezo the next morning, I could see the cascading foothills of the Picos de Europa mountains, their gray and brown limestone surfaces contrasting with the red tile roofs of the town of Potes. After eating a delicious hot breakfast including "frisuelos," a local dish made from fried batter topped with sugar, I loaded up the bike and rode north toward La Hermida.

I was immediately struck by how beautiful the sedimentary rock cliffs all around me were. As the road gently curved back and forth, following the Deva River, the silvery faces rose sharply on both sides, in many cases extending out into the road. Portions of the vertical surfaces were cut away to make room for traffic, and nets were in place to protect cars from falling rocks, creating a tunnel-like effect.

The jagged rocky cliffs along the Deva River in Spain towered high above me and often jutted out into the road, creating a canopy effect as I wound my way along the shoreline.

I continued north and east along the Pas River and a variety of narrow and pock-marked roads through small clusters of homes and businesses, past Vega de Pas and the little town of Yera, where a small sign warned motorists of sharp curves for the next ten kilometers. As the route rose in elevation, the valley to my right opened, and I was hit with an explosion of green— lime green meadows, hunter green foothills, olive green crops, and forest green trees, all undulating in waves below me with yellow wildflowers sprinkled along the sides of the road.

As I zigged and zagged up and down the mountain pass, I found the hairpin curves challenging enough to require my focus but not so demanding as to take away from the beauty of the surroundings. There was enough time between the tight twists to enjoy the road, and the surface of the pavement itself was in relatively good shape, with just enough room for two cars to safely pass one another. Reaching the bottom of the mountain pass, I laughed out loud with joy, feeling like a kid at an amusement park who has just gotten off a particularly thrilling roller coaster ride.

At the base of the mountain, after passing the town of Bercedo, I headed north and then east again into France, enjoying spectacular views of the Bay of Biscay, especially at Castro-Urdiales, where the gray-blue water rippled gently onto the orange-hued sand beach underneath jagged gray cliffs.

From my lodging in Bordeaux Lac, I headed north the next day to the UNESCO World Heritage Site of Mont-Saint-Michel, one of the most popular tourist destinations in France. Located between Normandy and Brittany, this gothic style Benedictine abbey and the walled village that grew up around it are considered a "wonder of the west." The site is striking because of its high walls and soaring church spire, as well as for its unique natural setting. Perched amid a vast sandbank, the village appears to rise from the ocean. As I rode my bike north toward the location, I was treated to a variety of spectacular views of the village jutting up into the sky over fields of grass, crops of corn, and then the sandy banks of the bay.

After parking in an authorized lot off the island, I took a shuttle to the village, where I wandered the cobblestone streets looking at the little shops and restaurants, climbed up the steps to explore the stone ramparts, and gazed out at the views of the sea and the beach. The highlight of my visit there was the omelet I ate at La Mere Poulard before leaving. The famous delicacies are made by whisking eggs in handmade copper bowls and then cooking them over an open fire.

I can't remember ever eating an omelet for dinner before. This world-famous delicacy, first created by Annette Poulard in 1873, served with shaved truffles and truffle oil and accompanied by a small pan of fried bacon and potatoes, was filled with flavor.

Perhaps it was because I was so hungry, but that breakfast I ate for dinner really hit the spot. The omelet, served along with a small pan of fried bacon and potatoes, was light and fluffy and reminded me of the soufflés my mom made for me as a child, with a thin crust on one side and rather foamy egg underneath. The fact that it was cooked in butter added a lot of flavor, as did the truffle oil that I generously applied. After polishing off every bite of the savory meal, I sat for a while enjoying the view of the village streets from my seat by the window. What an enchanting place to visit!

From my room in Montgomery near Mont Saint Michel, I rode north the next morning toward Normandy, enjoying the sunny weather and mild temperatures and taking in the views of cattle grazing contentedly in their fields. I passed fields of corn waving gently in the wind, and neatly rolled bales of hay dotted the countryside around me.

Arriving at Omaha Beach, I stopped to look at the stainless steel sculpture, Les Braves, commemorating the sacrifice the US 29th and 1st Infantry men made there during the D-Day invasion to help liberate France from the Nazis. Having been away from home for almost eight weeks at that point, it was especially emotional for me to reflect on the heroism of my country's soldiers and to see our flag flying proudly behind this monument. Although I do not come from a military family, it was moving to see our country's troops recognized for their bravery at such a historic site.

I rode several miles down the road to Pointe Du Hoc to see the ninety-foot cliffs that our US Army Rangers so bravely scaled when they attacked and captured this area, freeing the French people there from German control. It was gratifying to see how many tourists were visiting the area and to read the information about this important part of our history.

After spending some time at both beaches, I headed northeast to the coastal town of Le Tréport. Descending into the village, my jaw dropped as I took in a magnificent view of the bright blue waters of the English Channel, punctuated by the city's sheer, white, chalky cliffs rising above them. After spending some time in the bustling seaside resort, I continued east on a variety of scenic backroads before settling in for the night in Calais.

Looking at my map that night, I realized it wouldn't take much extra time to travel to both Belgium and the Netherlands on my way back to Germany. My visit to the wartime memorials for America's service people had heightened my sense of excitement about returning to my home country after months away. At the same time, I hoped to make every day left on my summer journey count, knowing I would not return for another such adventure until the next year. Intrigued with the idea of visiting the iconic windmills just south of Rotterdam and having the opportunity to travel through four European countries in one day, I headed north the next morning.

Gassing up in Belgium, I continued to the small town of Kinderdijk, passing a variety of dikes full of pedestrians and riders on scooters enjoying the fresh air and views of the reservoirs below them. Parking near the city's collection of nineteen eighteenth-century windmills, I strolled alongside a waterway filled with lily pads and small boats and lined with colorful flowers along its banks, gazing at the ancient brick structures with blades slowly rotating in the afternoon wind.

After admiring the views, I headed back down the main street to stop for lunch in town, ordering mustard soup and a fried croquette so I could sample something local. Satisfied by a good, hot lunch, I got back on the bike and headed south to Germany for the night.

With only one full riding day left before my departure from the Frankfurt airport two days later, I left Kamp Linfort, Germany, the next morning to head south to Heidelberg, following a route that led me along the Rhine River much of the way and traveling on the eastern side of the waterway to Rudesheim and beyond.

As I followed one gentle curve of the body of water after another in the hot afternoon sun, I had plenty of time to see the vineyards lined up in the foothills, castles perched on hilltops, and villages clustered in the valleys. Bicyclists pedaled along on the paths on one side of me, and trains whizzed by on the other. Looking out at Europe's busiest river, I could see barges carrying goods, ferries transporting cars, and pleasure boats holding gawking tourists on the upper decks.

When I pulled into Heidelberg that evening, I followed the winding path of the Neckar River on the northern side of town, enjoying views of the smooth, deep-green water sporting a variety of boats and arched brick bridges. Stone turrets of old castles stood in contrast to the hustle and bustle of cars and buses moving on the city roads, and throngs of locals and tourists walking along the riverbanks. I navigated along the cobblestone streets and past the aged buildings of Old Town before stopping to purchase breakfast supplies and snacks and settling into a motorcycle camp south of town, where I would leave Adventure Baby until my return the following June.

I spent the next day getting the bike ready for storage—removing anything I planned to take home with me, disconnecting the battery, and labeling the parts on it that needed to be repaired in my absence. I also re-packed my gear, placing the bulky items in a large duffel bag appropriate for the luggage compartment of the airplane. I put the smaller personal items into a. piece of motorcycle luggage that converted into a backpack I could wear as I traveled home. Although this was my first long-distance trip on an adventure bike and I was still learning how and what to pack on the road, I was pleased that my gear had held up well, that I had not forgotten any essential items, and that I was able to safely transport everything I needed, either with me in the passenger area of the airplane or stowed below in the cargo hold.

The next day I arranged for a ride to the airport, checked in my luggage, passed through airport security, and boarded the colorfully painted Icelandair plane that would take me to my connecting flight in Reykjavik back to America. When the aircraft, decorated with wavy blue and green images of the northern lights, lifted off the airport tarmac in Frankfurt, I leaned back in my seat, filled with a sense of gratitude for all I had learned and experienced during my summer travels. I closed my eyes and rested, knowing that for one of the few times in weeks I was not in charge of piloting the vehicle I was in.

My thoughts turned toward home, my heart soaring with joy at the prospect of seeing my friends and family, students, coworkers, tutoring clients, and neighbors again. Although my younger son, Elliot, who lived with me, was on his own vacation that week, we would be reconnecting in person soon, and I couldn't wait to give him a big hug and catch up with him. I was also looking forward to so many of the little things I had missed while abroad—speaking English with everyone I encountered, sleeping in my own bed, knowing where to find what I needed in the grocery store, and taking a shower with a washcloth and a bar of soap while using a shower head that didn't move while I used it.

It seemed fitting that the airplane that took me home after two months on the road in Europe sported the same green and blue artwork depicting the northern lights as the one that transported me from Portland to Iceland at the beginning of my journey.

CHAPTER 23

COMING FULL CIRCLE

After two uneventful flights, I arrived in Portland a little after six o'clock that night and passed through border control, walking out to meet Grant Myers at the baggage claim area where he had dropped me off two months earlier. As he smiled at me from inside his bright red pickup idling at the curb, his white mustache and hair highlighting his tanned cheeks and big grin, I felt a palpable sense of happiness, gratitude, and relief.

Safely back on US soil after two months overseas and being warmly welcomed by a friend who had supported me throughout my summer travels, I was hit with the magnitude of the obstacles I had recently overcome in my journey to Europe and back. It was hard for me to believe that after receiving such significant medical news in June, my bike and I had not only made it to Iceland but had traveled over 11,000 miles through twenty-two countries in sixty days.

As a middle-aged math teacher with almost no athletic ability, I never would have imagined I could battle death-defying winds and frigid temperatures while circumnavigating Iceland alone, forge my way up through Norway to the Arctic Ocean and the northernmost point of Europe, successfully steer my bike to safety while experiencing unexpected and potentially deadly mechanical issues, and find my way through so many unfamiliar places with different customs, languages, and currencies, including the outskirts of a NATO military base.

However, given what I had discovered over the last few years about the extent of God's grace and provision for me, it all somehow made sense. It wasn't that I was particularly talented or gifted but rather that I had learned to respond to obstacles by asking myself what I would do if fear were not my first thought and then trusting God to help me take those next steps. Instead of being paralyzed by fear for what might happen or shame about what had happened, I had been able to move forward with confidence, knowing that God would help me overcome an obstacle, embrace a difficulty, or pivot away from what might not be a wise course of action.

Sometimes this help came through the assistance of others. I had seen God's hand in the offer of monetary support from a retired Marine the day after I received an unexpected financial blow, in the presence of a tow truck operator parked in the gas station in front of me right when my bike's starter failed, and in the kindness of the doctors at OHSU who had given me the go-ahead to load my bike on the ship headed for Iceland in time for me to embark on such a wonderful European adventure.

Having come from such a place of fear and hopelessness just a few years earlier, I had a heightened sense of appreciation for the joy and peace that I now found possible, even in the face of new trials. Finding out before my trip that I had four tumors in my brain served to increase the fervency with which I was determined to live my life to the fullest, as I realized with even more clarity that I could not know how much longer I had on earth. None of us do. My interactions with others while abroad had helped me to reaffirm that nothing was more important than using whatever time I had left on earth to treat others with love and kindness.

Grateful for the peace and contentment I felt and hoping to inspire others to enjoy fuller lives in the face of fearful circumstances, I had resolved when I landed in Portland to spend the first few months I was home from my summer adventure writing a second book detailing the powerful lessons I had learned on the road in the years since I had written my first book, *Two-Wheeled Wind Therapy*. I hoped to finish the first draft by the end of December, freeing up more time for me to ride locally in the spring and making it possible for my publisher to get the new book out before my next planned summer trip by bike to Africa.

I didn't realize when I landed in Oregon that, rather than finishing my book in December, I would instead find myself returning to Europe at Christmas for one of the most meaningful experiences of my lifetime. Or that other decisions I made shortly after my return would also significantly reduce both my writing and riding time over the next several months, forcing me to adjust my expectations. It seemed that I would be living out the very lessons I had been learning—prioritizing relationships with my loved ones over time on the bike.

Having spent the night in so many warm and welcoming lodging accommodations over the summer, I returned to my unfinished house at the end of August, determined to create a fitting home environment for the holidays.

CHAPTER 24

HOME IS WHERE THE HEART IS

My first thought upon walking into my home in Portland after my trip was, "Where did all my furniture go?" I had finished a major remodel a year and a half before, laying down solid wood floors, installing new kitchen cupboards and appliances, replacing the orangish-stained baseboards and trim, hanging modern lighting, and converting a hideous indoor pond with a corrugated plastic ceiling into a tranquil workout room with a real ceiling featuring multiple skylights. Although I had spent months searching for discounted materials, shopped Black Friday deals, and bartered and traded, I had run out of money before the project was fully completed, leaving my house with two unfinished fireplaces and almost no furniture.

I had given away or sold almost all our existing living space furniture at the beginning of the construction project because the house needed to be emptied for the flooring to be laid, and it didn't seem to make sense to pay for several months of storage for all my ripped, broken, stained, and outdated seating, rugs, side tables, and lamps.

Having spent the night in so many different, yet welcoming, hostels, hotels, and guest houses over the course of my European adventure, I was struck anew by the starkness of my home when I first walked in. I had kept a kitchen table during the remodel and had managed to buy a few items of used furniture afterwards—two sofas, two armchairs, and one rug. But the house was barely utilitarian, with almost nothing on the walls or floors, no side tables or coffee tables, and few decorative accents.

I decided almost immediately after returning that I wanted to prioritize making my home more welcoming, even if it meant riding less and tutoring extra hours on the weekend. I knew that all three of my children would be home for both Thanksgiving and Christmas and resolved to finish as many of the remaining household projects by then as possible. I wanted Elliot to be able to enjoy our home more fully and for the other two children to feel even more comfortable relaxing and spending time together while visiting me.

Over the course of the next few months, I managed to finish both fireplaces, hang artwork in every room, install a second TV, purchase another area rug and several side tables, and procure more seating throughout the house. I even fixed the hot tub in our back yard that had been on its way out for years. Although I kept costs to a minimum by buying mostly secondhand items and using previously purchased materials for both fireplaces, the financial outlay was substantial, requiring me to tutor thirty hours a week on top of my full-time teaching job.

Although it was hard work to make such headway on the home and I did miss the lost time on the bike, it was also extremely gratifying to see everything coming together and to receive positive feedback from Elliot, my tutoring clients, and members of the singles group at my church wahen I hosted our weekly Bible studies or monthly social events. My guests told me that my home seemed light and cheerful and that they felt welcome. One of my Bible study members mentioned that spending time in my home was one of the highlights of the group experience for him.

On October 4, amid many of these projects, I was sitting at my desk at the high school between classes, thinking about which math lessons to work on next, when I noticed an email from my mother with the subject header "question." Having no idea what the email might be about, I clicked it open and was shocked to read the contents.

Apparently, my elderly grandmother in Switzerland had been asking to talk to me for me for the first time since she had been diagnosed with dementia and placed in the nursing home several years earlier. Her caregivers had conveyed my grandmother's wishes to my mom, who was checking to see what I would like to do.

My heart hammered in my chest and tears ran down my face as I read the message from my mother. I still felt acute pain from having been so near Grannie over the summer but not being able to see her. There was not even a second of doubt in my mind when I read the email that I wanted to call my grandmother at the first possible opportunity.

I had been advised by well-meaning friends and family that my grandmother might not know who I was, remember how to speak English, understand what I was saying, or even be awake enough to talk. I understood that all of these eventualities were possible but knew I would rather try to communicate with her than pass up an opportunity because it might not work out the way I wanted.

I had prayed to God that he would "open the door" for me to speak with my grandmother and felt certain that the email from my mom was an answer to prayer.

I had been learning so much about God's presence and provision in my life over the last several years, but the foundation for my faith had been laid when I was a young child. While I was growing up, my mom had exposed me to a wide variety of religions and encouraged me to make my own spiritual choices. Over the years, we had meditated with incense at Buddhist temples, ridden the streets of San Francisco looking for Catholic churches with different stained-glass windows, visited a Mormon temple, and temporarily become part of a Sunday school in a Presbyterian congregation.

I didn't end up making a commitment to any particular religion until my sophomore year in high school, after learning about Christianity through my best friend, Michelle. Interestingly enough, it wasn't so much the principles of the doctrine that attracted me but rather the way in which my friend acted out her convictions. I was captivated by her abundant kindness, unwavering unselfishness, and unbridled joy. Although I've experienced ups and downs in my own spiritual walk over the years since then, I have never doubted my choice in beliefs, partially because it had been my own from the very beginning.

The challenges of the last several years had helped strengthen the faith I had been developing since my teen years. But nothing could have prepared me for the magnitude and specificity of the way God answered my prayers about my grandmother.

After arrangements had been made with the administration of the nursing home, I called the front desk at my grandmother's facility before work just two days after receiving the email from my mother, not sure how the call would go but hoping for the best. I held my breath while the receptionist carried the phone to my grandmother's room, placed it next to her ear, and loudly announced who was on the phone.

I burst out in sobs the second my grandmother called me by name, delighted to hear her familiar melodic, high-pitched, perfectly enunciated and accented voice. Grasping my phone, I heaved great sighs of joy as she told me she had been waiting for my call and asked me to come visit her. Speaking mostly in English, she declared, "I would love to see you," and then she repeatedly assured me, "My door is not locked, just walk in." Not sure how I would make it happen but fully convinced there was nothing I wanted to do more, I exclaimed over and over to her, "I'm coming, Grannie. I love you. I'm coming."

It didn't really hit me until after I hung up the phone how miraculous the call had been on so many levels. My grandmother being awake, able to speak English, remembering who I was, calling me by name, and expressing a wish to see me were more than I could have hoped for. I would have elected to visit her under any circumstances. However, what really took my breath away was the fact she had chosen to tell me her door was unlocked after I had specifically prayed to God to open a door for me to see her. In my heart, I just knew the message had to be heaven sent.

I immediately turned to the task of setting up the logistics for a visit during my Christmas break, a feat that was no small matter, given the great distance and cost involved. I was already essentially working two full-time jobs to pay the contractors and wasn't sure how I would fund over $2,000 in airfare and $1,000 in lodging and food.

Thinking over my options, I decided to call the kind sponsor who had contributed funds toward my Iceland trip the previous year, tell him about the unexpected opportunity to see my grandmother, and ask if he would consider paying for my airfare to Switzerland. I had anticipated that he would need a while to think about my request, but before I could even finish my sentence, he cheerfully proclaimed, "I would be glad to help." Stunned by his generosity, I booked my flight shortly thereafter, arranging to leave the morning after classes ended and returning six days later, giving me five nights in Switzerland and a few days back at home to prepare for my children's arrival for the holidays.

The next few weeks passed quickly, with me praying daily that my grandmother would live long enough for me to see her and hug her one last time. At her advanced age, I knew it was possible she would pass before I arrived but desperately hoped that she would hold on until I got there.

My flight from Portland to Switzerland in mid-December did not go as expected. My late-night segment out of Dallas/ Forth Worth was delayed, and I missed my connection in London the following day. Upon arriving at Heathrow Airport, I was directed to the end of a long line of passengers waiting to re-book their flights. Remembering a tip I had read about handling such situations, I called the airline my flight was booked with while I was waiting in line so that they could save me a seat on the next plane to Geneva, a 4:15PM flight that would get me to Geneva just two-and-a-half hours later than originally planned.

Unfortunately, when I made it to the front of the line over an hour later, the agent there told me the flight I had a saved seat on did not exist. Although I begged them to find the flight and explained how important it was to me to see my grandmother, the agent and her supervisor insisted my only option was a plane that left after 6PM, putting me at my grandmother's nursing home after midnight.

Realizing I could not change their minds, I accepted the much later segment, hoping that I could use the boarding pass to make it through security to a gate agent who could change my reservation. After working my way through multiple terminals and checkpoints, I finally found the 4:15 flight I had a seat saved on, and a kind agent there gave me a new boarding pass. As the plane lifted off the tarmac, I sat back in relief and whispered, "I'm coming, Grannie, I'm coming."

Arriving in Geneva after seven o'clock at night, I cleared passport control, picked up a baguette with cheese and ham to go from a vendor at the terminal and ran along with my roller bag to the adjacent train station, managing to purchase a ticket for the forty-five-minute ride to Morges on a train that left just seconds after I boarded. Disembarking after 9PM, I called the nursing home to clarify their full business name so I could get directions in my navigation app for the half-mile walk there.

The person who answered asked who I was visiting and when I was arriving. Concerned that they might tell me not to come so late, I decided to hang up without answering their question. It wasn't like me to take such rash action, but at that point I was resolved not to let anything keep me from being reunited with my grandmother as soon as possible. Despite the late hour, I was determined to do everything I could to see her that night, knowing I would always regret it if I waited until morning and she ended up passing before then.

As I raced along the deserted city streets in the just-above-freezing temperatures and pulling my luggage behind me, my hands became numb, and my nose started running in the moist air. Racing up to the facility just before 10PM, I found the main door locked and could see no one at the front counter. I called the nursing home on my phone again, this time hopeful that once they saw me standing there, they would let me in.

A kind nurse opened the door for me and led me down the antiseptic hallway. As I walked toward my grandmother's room, I gasped for air, out of breath from running and overcome with emotion about finally seeing my Grannie after ten years apart. I didn't know what to expect, as I had been told that she was in poor condition, given her age and medical condition.

However, when the door opened and I saw her lying in her bed, she looked every bit as beautiful to me as she always had, her combed ash blond hair fanning out on her pillow, fine porcelain skin pink and moist, inked eyebrows perfectly shaped, and lips still carefully outlined in permanent color. She was resting peacefully in a pink nightgown with her hands clasped on top of the blankets covering her chest.

Because she was blind and almost deaf, I wasn't sure how to let her know I was there. Instinctively, I reached out to touch her hands with my ice-cold fingers. Her eyes opened, and she exclaimed in French, "You are so cold! You poor thing." She started rubbing my hands gently between hers, even placing them under her covers and against her upper chest to help me warm up. Although my grandmother did not yet know it was me, I sobbed with gratitude for the opportunity to feel her and hear her voice. My tears were streaming freely down my cheeks.

My extremities began to return to room temperature, and I carefully massaged Grannie's hands back, wanting to gently convey to her without words how much I loved her. As I continued to rub her fingers, palms, and forearms, she sighed with contentment, raising her arms higher and turning her hands back and forth to show me where she wanted the pressure applied.

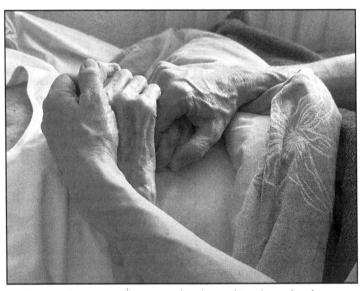

During the many walks my grandmother and I took together during my lifetime, we typically clasped each other's hands, shaking them three times in a row to signify we loved each other. During my visit with her at age 105, I was grateful to be able to gently clasp her hands in mine and signal my love to her in the same manner.

Hoping that somehow I had comforted my grandmother, I leaned down close to her ear, as the nurse had demonstrated to me earlier, and loudly declared, "Grannie, it's me—Kathleen." "Who?" she asked. "Kathleen. Your granddaughter. I love you so much!" As I finished speaking, I grasped her hands in mine and gently pressed them together while shaking them back and forth three times, something she and I had always done to show our affection while walking or speaking together. Grannie's eyes opened even wider, and she enthusiastically shook my hands back three times, proclaiming, "And I love you!"

I stayed with Grannie well into the night, massaging her, giving her water from a cup with a spout, and gently feeding her very small pieces of banana by placing them delicately inside her mouth. Afterward, as I walked back through the cold night air to my now-closed hotel to do a late-night self-check-in, I felt an indescribable peace, knowing that whatever happened next, I had had the opportunity to convey my love and care to my grandmother one last time. All the running around inside airports, changes to previously made plans, and logistical hurdles had been worth it.

Over the next several days, I walked to Grannie's nursing home first thing in the morning and stayed there with her until after her dinner, feeding her meals, massaging her, adjusting her hospital bed, and telling her repeatedly how much I loved her.

Grannie had told me many times over a period of years about how she had comforted my grandfather when he was dying, explaining to me that the sense of touch was the last thing to go, and describing how she had lovingly stroked his hands. I had benefited so much over my lifetime from the wisdom that my grandmother had imparted to me, but it never occurred to me that the stories she told me about ministering to her husband would help me to understand how to show her my love as she herself was nearing the end of her life.

Although Grannie's ability to understand who I was seemed to vary hour to hour, day to day, and even minute to minute, she always responded positively to me grasping her hands and shaking them back and forth the way we had always done, opening her eyes wider, shaking my hands back, thanking me, sighing with contentment, and telling me she loved me. What a gift it was to both of us to be able to communicate.

On impulse, during my last night with her, I decided to use one hand to videotape our exchange, managing to capture on my phone me telling my grandmother how much I loved her and her ardently proclaiming, "And I love you too!" and then making a joyful sigh. What a priceless gift!

Several well-meaning people who had known Grannie for many years had cautioned me before my trip that it might be disturbing to me to see my grandmother in her weakened, frail, and dementia-riddled state. After they had spent time with her in the nursing home, they had experienced difficulty reconciling her changed condition with the memories of the person they had known her to be in the past.

In my case, however, the trip had been hugely therapeutic. Although I knew that Grannie's lack of short-term memory would most likely not allow her to remember my visit, I was comforted that I had brought her joy while I was with her and that she and I had been able to express our affection for each other one last time. I was also grateful to have a sense of closure, knowing that I had come when she asked for me and that I had been able to say goodbye to her in person.

My trip back to Portland was rather eventful, with missed connections, a cancelled flight, mechanical issues, a delayed flight, and a rather heroic effort on Swiss International Airlines' part to find a way to get me home in time for the holidays with my children. Although I was exhausted from working my way through so many different terminals, airports, and airplanes, nothing could dampen the sense of joy and gratitude that I felt about my trip.

Arriving back in Portland, I shifted my focus toward preparing for Christmas—shopping for holiday meal ingredients, wrapping presents, cleaning the house, hanging more artwork on the walls, and attending an inspiring candlelight Christmas Eve service at my church.

Ethan, Elliot, and Eleanor had spent Christmas Day with their father and arrived in Portland on December 26, giving us a full week together before I went back to work and Ethan and Eleanor returned to California. The next several days were filled with priceless moments as we shared a family meal with my mother and brother, walked on the trails near the Willamette River, went out to eat, and relaxed in our newly finished family and living rooms.

Each Christmas since the children were little, I have asked them to write me a note or letter expressing positive sentiments as their main Christmas present to me. I have always felt that hearing kind words from them was more valuable to me than any store-bought gift would be. When they were quite young, the notes were relatively short and often misspelled but always touching. As the children matured, the letters became lengthier and more eloquent and often, particularly with my daughter, accompanied by endearing art sketches of our life together.

This Christmas, when I opened my letters from the children, it was as if each one of them was a validation of the positive life choices I had made as I had matured and grown in my faith over the previous few months and years. My son, Ethan, wrote, "I really appreciate how devoted you are as a parent. Especially lately how you've made it a point to ask how we can connect and communicate better—it makes me feel loved and heard." What a gift. I can't think of anything Ethan could have said that would have meant more to me, as I was so very grateful that we had recently grown closer together again after the struggles we had gone through four years before.

Elliot commented, "It means a lot to me how supportive you are of me both from an emotional standpoint as well as making sure I always have a loving home to stay in. I find it impressive how you always find a way to stay positive in any situation, and that is certainly something that I try and aim for in my life. Additionally, I find it very impressive how hard you work in order to provide an amazing home for your family, and this is the type of mindset I want to have when I eventually start a family." My heart swelled when I read Elliot's words. There is no higher praise for me than one of my children aspiring to emulate me. Elliot has been a consistent source of strength, comfort, and assistance during the time that he has lived with me. It was encouraging to hear that he felt the way he did and especially affirming that he recognized and valued the sacrifices I had made to create a more welcoming home environment since returning from my European trip.

Eleanor gifted me with a card including a hand-drawn image of me heading up a winding mountain road on my motorcycle with the sun shining above me. Her kind sentiments included that she was " . . . thankful that we've had more time to call and catch up with each other this last year—whether it's on our morning walks or a random weekend." She added, "Your determination after you've set a goal for yourself is truly an unstoppable force . . . I'm sure in this next year you'll make sure to climb higher mountains and reach the top of wherever you set your sights. You deserve all the joy and fulfillment you and your bike can carry throughout this next year."

My soul soared with delight that my beautiful, precious daughter had not only recognized the determination with which I was pursuing living my life to the fullest but had also acknowledged the priority I had made to connect with her while amid those pursuits.

As I sat in my recently completed living room, surrounded by my children and the vestiges of all our Christmas wrapping paper with bows scattered all around, it occurred to me that the loving notes I had received were the most priceless gifts of all. Holding their precious cards in my hands and taking in the holiday setting, I reflected on how grateful I was for that very moment.

Celebrating Christmas with my children and other loved ones over the holidays helped me to appreciate the extent to which I had strengthened my relationships with them as I had grown and matured as an individual.

The difficulties the children and I had experienced together over the last several years were in the past. The discovery of my brain tumors just a few months before had helped me to better understand that I could not predict what the future would hold for the children and me or even how many more Christmases we would have together. But the kind sentiments they expressed to me on paper helped me rest in the assurance that I had managed to convey the breadth and depth of my love for them through my words and actions. I could think of nothing more important I could do with the life I had left than to show them and other loved ones how much I cared.

As a younger woman, I would not have predicted that my middle-aged years would end up being so tumultuous or challenging, that mistakes I made and challenges I faced would result in so much pain. But I could now see that the obstacles I had overcome, while daunting, had forged me into becoming a woman of inner strength and confidence. As I learned to live in the moment, be open to adventure, and face fear from a perspective of power, I was not only maturing and developing as a person but also strengthening relationships with those around me. Although the choices I had made since returning home from Europe had meant less time on the road and delaying the completion of my book by several weeks, I could think of nothing more important than prioritizing life with my family. I was finally learning to live life at full throttle.

ACKNOWLEDGEMENTS

The process of "birthing" a book is somewhat like that of undertaking a move—when you reach out to others for help in the process, you often gain more insight into the nature of your relationships with friends and loved ones. With so many of us leading such busy lives, it speaks volumes when someone you care about takes time out of their day to provide feedback on an idea, assist with a technical issue, suggest an editing adjustment, publicly lend their support, affirm your choices, or add to your visual impact.

I am so grateful to my three beautiful children, Ethan, Elliot, and Eleanor, for not only giving me the courage to face my fears but also for cheering me on as I have grown and developed through the process. My life has been immeasurably blessed by their presence.

Mike Fitterling at Road Dog Publications graciously offered again to bring my manuscript to print, freeing up more time for me to focus on living out what I was writing.

Perhaps the most significant contributors to this volume were my dear friends Kathy Nesper and Jena Starkes.

As a close confidant for over twenty-five years, Kathy has come alongside me as I faced all the challenges that I have written about—lending a listening ear, giving me her perspective on my situation, and encouraging me spiritually. In addition to delivering timely and sage advice, Kathy was responsible for editing all the grammar and punctuation in my manuscript, wordsmithing, teaching me how to utilize a variety of technical resources, and working tirelessly to help me tie up loose ends, significantly elevating the professionalism of the final product. I would not be the person I write about today without her unconditional love and support.

Jena breezed into my world like a breath of fresh air when I first contacted her for website support in the process of writing *Two-Wheeled Wind Therapy*. As an articulate, technically gifted, no-nonsense New Yorker, she can always be counted on to tell me like it is, even if it isn't what I hope to hear. Jena brought all her remarkable skills to bear again this time in helping me to craft the direction and content of my writing, develop a following on my website, and seek out speaking engagements. She is the genius behind this book's cover, creating a vibrant and relevant representation of what I dearly hope to share with my readers.

I am humbled that four-time Olympian Ruben Gonzales, National President of the Women's Motorcycle Association Michelle Lamphere, and co-host of Adventure Rider Radio RAW Sam Manicom all graciously offered to lend their public support of *Living at Full Throttle*, crafting relevant and impactful endorsements for the back cover.

Much of what is written in this volume is brought to life through the stories of adventure from my time on the road, all of which is made more possible by the support and encouragement of two fellow motorcyclists, Grant Myers and Allen Nay. Grant and Allen both served along with Kathy as my US "pit crew" for my summer 2023 journey, providing around-the-clock assistance when called upon. On one particularly notable occasion, Grant managed to talk me through the mechanics of fixing my handlebar navigation mount when it fell apart on the side of the road in Poland. Allen's prayer support and willingness to listen was much appreciated as I thought through a variety of challenging circumstances when calling him from all corners of Europe.

Finally, I'd like to thank my best friend, Michelle Martin, for being an unwavering source of love and comfort through over four decades of ups and downs, joyfully and generously helping me to live my life more fully.

Also from Road Dog Publications

Those Two Idiots![1][2] by A. P. Atkinson
Mayhem, mirth, and adventure follow two riders across two continents. Setting off for Thailand thinking they were prepared, this story if full of mishaps and triumphs. An honest journey with all the highs and lows, wins and losses, wonderful people and low-lifes, and charms and pitfalls of the countries traveled through.

Motorcycles, Life, and . . . [1][2] by Brent Allen
Sit down at a table and talk motorcycles, life and . . . (fill in the blank) with award winning riding instructor and creator of the popular "Howzit Done?" video series, Brent "Capt. Crash" Allen. Here are his thoughts about riding and life and how they combine told in a lighthearted tone.

The Elemental Motorcyclist[1][2] by Brent Allen
Brent's second book offers more insights into life and riding and how they go together. This volume, while still told in the author's typical easy-going tone, gets down to more specifics about being a better rider.

A Short Ride in the Jungle[1][2] by Antonia Bolingbroke-Kent
A young woman tackles the famed Ho Chi Minh Trail alone on a diminutive pink Honda Cub armed only with her love of Southeast Asia, its people, and her wits.

Bonneville Go or Bust[1][2] by Zoë Cano
A true story with a difference. Zoë had no experience for such a mammoth adventure of a lifetime but goes all out to make her dream come true to travel solo across the lesser known roads of the American continent on a classic motorcycle.

I loved reading this book. She has a way of putting you right into the scene. It was like riding on the back seat and experiencing this adventure along with Zoë. —★★★★ Amazon Review

Southern Escapades[1][2] by Zoë Cano

As an encore to her cross country trip, Zoë rides along the tropical Gulf of México and Atlantic Coast in Florida, through the forgotten backroads of Alabama and Georgia. This adventure uncovers the many hidden gems of lesser known places in these beautiful southern states.

. . . Zoë has once again interested and entertained me with her American adventures. Her insightful prose is a delight to read and makes me want to visit the same places.—★★★★★ Amazon Review

Chilli, Skulls & Tequila[1][2] by Zoë Cano

Zoe captures the spirit of beautiful Baja California, México, with a solo 3 000 mile adventure encountering a myriad of surprises along the way and unique, out-of-the-way places tucked into Baja's forgotten corners.

Zoe adds hot chilli and spices to her stories, creating a truly mouth-watering reader's feast!—★★★★ Amazon Review

Hellbent for Paradise[1][2] by Zoë Cano

The inspiring—and often nail-biting—tale of Zoë's exploits roaming the jaw-dropping natural wonders of New Zealand on a mission to find her own paradise.

Mini Escapades around the British Isles[1][2] by Zoë Cano

As a wonderful compilation of original short stories closer to home, Zoë Cano captures the very essence of Britain's natural beauty with eclectic travels she's taken over the years exploring England, Ireland, Scotland, and Wales.

Shiny Side Up[1][2] by Ron Davis

A delightful collection of essays and articles from Ron Davis, Associate Editor and columnist for *BMW Owners News*. This book is filled with tales of the road and recounts the joys and foibles of motorcycle ownership and maintenance. Read it and find out why Ron is a favorite of readers of the *Owners News*!

Rubber Side Down[1][2] by Ron Davis
More great stuff from Ron Davis.

"[Ron] shares his experiences with modesty and humor, as one who is learning as he goes along. Which is what we all do in real life. And he does what all the best motorcycle writing does: he makes you wonder why you aren't out there riding your own bike, right now . . . his work simply helps you stay sane until spring."
—Peter Egan, *Cycle World* Columnist and author of *Leanings 1, 2,* and *3,* and *The Best of Peter Egan.*

Beads in the Headlight [1] by Isabel Dyson
A British couple tackle riding from Alaska to Tierra del Fuego two-up on a 31 year-old BMW "airhead." Join them on this epic journey across two continents.

A great blend of travel, motorcycling, determination, and humor.—★★★★★ Amazon Review

Chasing America [1][2] by Tracy Farr
Tracy Farr sets off on multiple legs of a motorcycle ride to the four corners of America in search of the essence of the land and its people.

In Search of Greener Grass [1] by Graham Field
With game show winnings and his KLR 650, Graham sets out solo for Mongolia & beyond. Foreword by Ted Simon

Eureka [1] by Graham Field
Graham sets out on a journey to Kazahkstan only to realize his contrived goal is not making him happy. He has a "Eureka!" moment, turns around, and begins to enjoy the ride as the ride itself becomes the destination.

Different Natures [1] by Graham Field
The story of two early journeys Graham made while living in the US, one north to Alaska and the other south through México. Follow along as Graham tells the stories in his own unique way.

Thoughts on the Road[1][2] *by Michael Fitterling*
The Editor of *Vintage Japanese Motorcycle Magazine* ponders his experiences with motorcycles and riding and how they've intersected and influenced his life.

Northeast by Northwest[1][2] *by Michael Fitterling*
The author finds two motorcycle journeys of immense help staving off depression and the other effects of stress. Along the way, he discovers the beauty of North America and the kindness of its people.
  . . . one of the most captivating stories I have read in a long time. Truly a MUST read!!—★★★★★ Amazon Review

A Year in Motion[1][2] *by Michael Fitterling*
After recovery from a long string of injuries, the author is determined to not let age or his damaged body hold him back. As soon as the doctors allow him, he gets back on the road. In that year, almost 24,000 miles roll under the wheels of his Tiger as he rides across the US. These are the stories of that year in motion.

Hit the Road, Jac![1][2] *by Jacqui Furneaux*
At 50, Jacqui leaves her home and family, buys a motorcycle in India, and begins a seven-year world-wide journey with no particular plan. Along the way she comes to terms with herself and her family.

Asphalt & Dirt[1][2] *by Aaron Heinrich*
A compilation of profiles of both famous figures in the motorcycle industry and relatively unknown people who ride, dispelling the myth of the stereotypical "biker" image.

The Dog, The Hog, & the Iron Horse[1][2] *by Alex Kendall*
An Englishman seeks out the "real" America and Americans on three trips across the US; one by bus, east to west; another by train west to east; and finally on an iconic Harley-Davidson motorcycle from north to south. Inspired by "beat" writers, join Alex on his exploration of this land of Kerouac and Thompson.

Chasing Northern Lights[1][2] *by Miguel Oldenberg*
A Venezuelan immigrant sets out to get to know his new country on the motorcycle ride of a lifetime.

The Tom Report [1] [2] by Tom Reuter
Two young men set out from Washington state on Suzuki DR650 dual sport motorcycles. Join them and a colorful cast of fellow travelers as they wind their way south to the end of the world. Their journey is filled with fun, danger, and even enlightenment.

Motorcycles, Minotaurs, & Banjos [1] [2] by Steven Sherrill
From the acclaimed author of five novels, one nominated for a Pulitzer (*Visits From the Drowned Girl*), comes Steven's first non-fiction work. This is a tale about his travels through Appalachia on a quest to visit the graves of his Old Time Folk Music banjo heroes on his motorcycle with his own banjo strapped across the back.

A Tale of Two Dusters & Other Stories [1] [2] by Kirk Swanick
In this collection of tales, Kirk Swanick tells of growing up a gearhead behind both the wheels of muscle cars and the handlebars of motorcycles and describes the joys and trials of riding.

Two-Wheeled Wind Therapy [1] [2] by Kathleen Terner
This memoir describes Kathleen's first solo cross-country trip and how it helped her learn to experience joy and hope again after surviving throat cancer, a second divorce, and teaching through the pandemic. Traveling over 15,000 miles through twenty-eight different states she began to see that her past may have shaped her but did not need to define her.

Man in the Saddle [1] [2] by Paul van Hoof
Aboard a 1975 Moto Guzzi V7, Paul starts out from Alaska for Ushuaia. Along the way there are many twists and turns, some which change his life forever. English translation from the original Dutch.

Distributed by:
NBN
national book network
Road Dog PUBLICATIONS
www.roaddogpub.com
Also available for [1] Kindle from amazon.com & [2] Nook from bn.com